The Naked Roommate's •First Year• SURVIVAL WORKBOOK

The **Ultimate Tools** for a **College Experience** with **More Fun**, **Less Stress**, and **Top Success**

2nd Edition

Harlan Cohen and Cynthia Jenkins Ph.D.

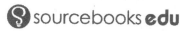
sourcebooks edu

Published by Sourcebooks EDU, an imprint of Sourcebooks, Inc.
P.O. Box 4410, Naperville, Illinois 60567-4410
(630) 961-3900
Fax: (630) 961-2168
www.sourcebooks.com

Printed and bound in the United States of America.
POD 10 9 8 7 6 5 4

Contents

Welcome to the Naked Workbook

If you're reading this, I assume that high school is behind you (or almost behind you) and college is now in front of you. While you worked hard to get into college along with your high school counselors, parents, and teachers, staying in college and having the best college experience is now entirely in your own hands.

I assume you are familiar with *The Naked Roommate* book, right? If not, please stop reading and find one. I'll put in a line break to give you time to locate and page through a copy of *The Naked Roommate*.

Welcome back!

So now that you've read *The Naked Roommate* (or pretended to read it) you're ready for the workbook. This workbook is designed to be a naked companion to *The Naked Roommate* book. Meaning, without *The Naked Roommate* book, this workbook will not have a companion (kind of sad). It's important to be familiar with *The Naked Roommate* book. (It's the equivalent to a toilet seat in the residence hall without a protective covering of toilet paper—it's not a good idea to do one without the other.) While *The Naked Roommate* book shares tips and stories of students living life in college, *The Naked Roommate's First Year Survival Workbook* is a place for you to create, map out, and live your own college experience.

I hope you enjoy this workbook and dive into it for class or on your own. I encourage you to become one with this workbook. I encourage you to even tear pages out of the workbook, so you can keep the important things you've written or post meaningful insights around your room, or keep them in your purse or wallet. Or, if you find that you are ever short on underwear and *really* want to become one with this workbook, these pages can also be used as a protective lining for a second or third wearing.

Disclaimer: these pages have not been tested as a liner for underwear on people or animals. Use at your own discretion.

I want to be clear—this is a workbook. That means this book involves doing some work. It's not like other books that are made for looking at words. This book is intended to be worked in. That means you can write in it, draw in it, make lists in it, create your research paper outline in it, tear out pages, and deface it (if you don't like the work you did in it). Yet, while this book is intended for work, this workbook shouldn't require that much work in order for you to get something out of it. If anything, this really should be called a "Not a Lot of Work Book," but that's just not something anyone calls a workbook, and it might slip through the cracks. Besides, that would diminish the power of the work and what you will accomplish by doing the work in this workbook.

If you look on the cover of this workbook (flip to the cover), you'll see the name Cynthia Jenkins. This is not my alter ego or other personality (my other personality's name is Harlannah Cohenconowitz). Cynthia and I bumped into each other several years ago when I discovered she had been using *The Naked Roommate* as a required text for the thousand-plus students enrolled in the first year experience course at the University of Texas at Dallas. After several conversations, meetings, and years of hearing about the amazing work happening in her instructors' classrooms, we decided to team up for this project. Cynthia is a passionate expert who encourages "naked" learning and student success.

I hope you enjoy this workbook. I hope it helps. If you do even a little bit of work in here, I promise your college experience will not just meet your expectations, it will *exceed* your expectations. And if you don't have expectations, even better; it will help you define them and then exceed them. Cynthia and I look forward to being here with you as you create your college experience. As always, you can email me at Harlan@HelpMeHarlan.com, find me on Facebook (www.Facebook.com/HelpMeHarlan and www.Facebook.com/TNRfanpage), on Twitter (@HarlanCohen and @NakedRoommate), and sitting on my couch eating.

And now, the "not a lot of work" part begins.

Thank you!

Harlan and Cynthia

A Special Note to Instructors

A Note to Instructors and Facilitators

Welcome instructors and facilitators. It's a pleasure to meet you!

Whether you're teaching a college-level first year experience course, a high school course for college-bound seniors, conducting a workshop for staff, or using this workbook as an ice-breaker, I hope this workbook will become a valuable resource and companion to *The Naked Roommate* book. In addition to this workbook, I should mention that there is also an instructor's guide available. The guide has detailed information on how to use this workbook and *The Naked Roommate* as a primary text or supplemental text. You can find out more information on the instructor's guide by visiting www.NakedRoommate.com and www.Facebook.com/TNRfanpage. You can also contact Sourcebooks or contact me (Harlan@HelpMeHarlan.com) or Cynthia (Cynthia@college-by-design.com) via email.

On another note, I should also mention that a fully updated edition of my book for parents was recently released: *The Naked Roommate: For Parents Only*. Think of it as "The Naked Parent" (but don't think about naked parents). I hope between the book, workbook, instructor's guide, and parent book, you'll have enough materials to help your students (and their parents) have an amazing college experience.

One final note: I'm always looking for feedback. In fact, I depend on it to make books as useful and valuable as possible. Your feedback is important and appreciated. Cynthia and I would love to hear what we can do to make this workbook even better. Please send feedback, comments, and suggestions to the email previously mentioned or via Facebook (www.Facebook.com/HelpmeHarlan and www.Facebook.com/TNRfanpage) or visit my websites www.HelpMeHarlan.com, www.NakedRoommate.com, and www.NakedRoommateForParents.com.

Thank you,

Harlan and Cynthia

NAKED PREPARATION

The Work before the Workbook

The 90/10 Rule

College is 90 percent amazing and 10 percent
difficult (or 10 percent BS). The secret is to NEVER let
the 10 percent take up 100 percent of your time.

The 90/10 rule is based on the premise that college is approximately 90 percent amazing and 10 percent difficult (or 10 percent BS). The problem is that too often, the 10 percent difficult can take up 100 percent of your time. This workbook will help make the 10 percent much more manageable and far less consuming.

To keep the 10 percent from getting out of control, you need to start by making some promises to yourself. Go through the list of promises that follows, and put an X next to the promises that you will make to yourself as you begin your college journey. Try not to lie to yourself (lying to yourself is always so sad). And please take your time.

I, _____, promise to

_____ be kind to myself

_____ be patient with myself

_____ be kind to classmates, roommates, and friends

_____ be patient with classmates, roommates, and friends

_____ give myself time to get comfortable with the uncomfortable

_____ work to find my place(s) on campus

_____ reach out for help before I need it

_____ try to have conversations, not confrontations

_____ make smart choices

_____ appreciate my imperfections

_____ follow my heart

_____ take chances in order to discover my passion

_____ give people permission to NOT always like me

_____ give professors permission to NOT know me

_____ not judge people until I can get to know them

_____ allow myself to NOT know the answer

_____ allow myself to be homesick at times

_____ allow myself to have fun without feeling guilty

_____ not allow significant others to define me and my choices

_____ listen to my parents even if I don't do what they say

_____ work to discover my passion

_____ get to know myself better

_____ get to know people who are different from me

_____ attend classes (as much as possible)

_____ get help if someone I know or am with needs it (regardless of the consequences)

_____ enjoy every moment—the good, the bad, and the uncomfortable

_____ find support on or near campus

_____ work to be my personal best

Add any of your own here.

_____ _____

_____ _____

_____ _____

Thank you for participating in the previous Naked Exercise. It's easy to lose sight of what this experience is about—YOU. Because so much of this workbook focuses on navigating through the difficult times that can come up in college, I want to make sure the positive amazing parts jump out.

Now, to accentuate the positive, I'd like for you to list ninety things that will make your college experience amazing. Ninety?! Yes, I'm serious. And no, I'm not on crack. (Why would you even think such a terrible thing? Speaking of crack, never do crack.) I'm really asking you to list ninety things that will make college life amazing.

Asking you to list nine things would be a waste of your time. That doesn't take much thought. Listing ninety means actually having to take the time to think about how much you have to look forward to in college. You might hate me now, but you'll appreciate this later (or you will never appreciate this or me). If you really can't list ninety right now, then you can always go back to this list later and add more things when you think of them. If you're doing this in a big group, suggest everyone offer their ideas (but no repeating).

I don't care what you list. You can talk about how much you'll love the weather, the glow of the football stadium at night, all your new freedom, the new food, dating, relationships, hooking up, staying a virgin, praying you stay a virgin, etc.—just list ninety things that you're looking forward to.

Ninety things I'm going to LIKE or even LOVE about college:
Write ninety things you're going to love about college...

1. _____

2. _____

3. _____

4. _____

5. _____

6. _____

7. _____

8. _____

9. _____

10. _____

11. _____

12. _____

13. _____

14. _____

15. _____

16. _____

17. _____

18. _____

19. _____

20. _____

21. _____

22. _____

23. _____

24. _____

25. _____

26. _____

27. _____

28. _____

29. _____

30. _____

You're one-third of the way there...

31. _____

32. _____

33. _____

34. _____

35. _____

36. _____

37. _____

38. _____

39. _____

40. _____

41. _____

42. _____

43. _____

44. _____

45. _____

You're halfway home. Dig deep. Don't forget to breathe.

46. _____

47. _____

48. _____

49. _____

50. _____

51. _____

52. _____

53. _____

54. _____

55. _____

56. _____

57. _____

58. _____

59. _____

60. _____

Almost there. Don't give up. Here, I'll help with one...

61. Not having to write ninety things I love about college again. ____

62. _____

63. _____

64. _____

65. _____

66. _____

67. _____

68. _____

69. _____

70. _____

71. _____

72. _____

73. _____

74. _____

75. _____

76. _____

77. _____

78. _____

79. _____

80. _____

81. _____

82. _____

83. _____

84. _____

85. _____

86. _____

87. _____

88. _____

89. _____

90. _____

Just in case you think of something else, I've included four extra lines.

91. _____

92. _____

93. _____

94. _____

Rate using a scale of 1–10.

> **1** = Not true → **5** = Somewhat true → **10** = Doesn't get any truer

_____ I know what life will be like in college.

_____ My expectations about college come from reliable sources, such as current students, recent college grads, a sibling in college, or an advisor.

_____ I make friends very quickly, so I will probably make friends in college fast.

_____ I am certain that my boyfriend or girlfriend from high school will stay my boyfriend or girlfriend while I'm in college.

_____ I am confident that I will get good grades in college (at least as good as I got in high school).

_____ I have no idea how I'll find my place(s) in college.

_____ I know exactly where I'll find my place(s) in college.

_____ I don't know what it means to "find my place(s)" in college.

_____ Time management freaks me out (not sure when or how I'll study).

_____ I'm afraid of getting lost on campus.

_____ I am completely comfortable being exactly who I am.

_____ I'm excited to become someone different in college.

_____ My parents are clueless about life in college.

_____ I'm worried about my parents being too involved in the choices I make.

_____ I plan to talk to/text/email my parents several times a week.

_____ I plan to talk to/text/email my parents several times a day.

_____ I'm concerned about getting homesick.

_____ I would rather text someone about a problem instead of talking about it.

Naked Exercise #1

Expect the Unexpected

You might think you know what will happen in college, but really, until you get there, you can't know. Start your college experience with expectations, but leave room to expect the unexpected.

Before buying your books and heading off to college, there's something you need to do. Identify your expectations.

Everyone has them. Even people who expect nothing have expectations because expecting nothing means expecting something because nothing is something.

Whatever you're expecting, make sure your expectations are realistic, that they are based on valid and trusted sources—not fictional sources (like an imaginary friend or Santa Claus or a hallucination). For example, are you relying on advice from a drugged out ex-student who failed out and then posted advice in a random college forum while in a fit of anger? That's not someone you should probably listen to. On the other hand, a teaching assistant who has spent three years on campus working with the dean of the department is likely to be a trusted source.

When creating expectations, there are three areas to examine:

- Academic expectations
- Social expectations
- Emotional expectations

Think about your expectations in these three areas of your life on campus, and enter them into the spaces on the following pages.

Naked Academic Expectations
(Majors, Grades, Professors, Graduation, Etc.)

Sample:

I expect to _skip classes and get a 4.0 GPA._

My source: _Drunk guy at a taco stand who claimed to have a 4.0 before vomiting on sidewalk._

Is this a reliable source? YES /(NO)

* * *

I expect to _____

My source: _____

Is this a reliable source? YES / NO

* * *

I expect to _____

My source: _____

Is this a reliable source? YES / NO

* * *

I expect to _____

My source: _____

Is this a reliable source? YES / NO

* * *

I expect to _____

My source: _____

Is this a reliable source? YES / NO

* * *

I expect to _____

My source: _____

Is this a reliable source? YES / NO

Naked Social Life Expectations
(Friends, Dating, Relationships, Sex Souvenirs, Etc.)

Sample:

I expect to <u>hook up at least seven times during the first seven days on campus.</u>

My source: <u>A YouTube video by a guy who hooked up with seven people in seven days.</u>

Is this a reliable source? YES / (NO)

* * *

I expect to _____

My source: _____

Is this a reliable source? YES / NO

* * *

I expect to _____

My source: _____

Is this a reliable source? YES / NO

* * *

I expect to _____

My source: _____

Is this a reliable source? YES / NO

* * *

I expect to _____

My source: _____

Is this a reliable source? YES / NO

* * *

I expect to _____

My source: _____

Is this a reliable source? YES / NO

Naked Emotional Life Expectations (Good Times, Bad Times, Homesickness, Etc.)

Sample:

I expect to *have the best year of my life.* _____

My source: *The movie Old School.* _____

Is this a reliable source? YES / (NO)

* * *

I expect to _____

My source: _____

Is this a reliable source? YES / NO

* * *

I expect to _____

My source: _____

Is this a reliable source? YES / NO

* * *

I expect to _____

My source: _____

Is this a reliable source? YES / NO

* * *

I expect to _____

My source: _____

Is this a reliable source? YES / NO

✎ Naked Journal #1: Your Naked Imagination

About these journal entries: you'll need to grab a pen and paper (or laptop or tablet) to do your journaling. Sure, I could have provided blank pages at the end of this workbook to do your naked journaling, but that would just make the workbook look bigger and no one needs to make this workbook look like more work.

Welcome to your first Naked Journal. Throughout the workbook you will be asked to do some writing. The Naked part of this has nothing to do with wearing clothing while writing your entries (please wear clothing when journaling in class or in public spaces; feel free to journal without clothing in private spaces). It's all about getting to the raw, uncensored, and honest truth at the core. Some journal entries will ask you to reflect, some will ask you to do some research, and others will ask you to talk to experts who have the information. All of this will help you to find the truth about life in college and what you want to get out of it.

For this journal entry, imagine you have access to a time machine (yes, I know time machines don't exist). Now imagine getting inside and traveling to your future. It's now college graduation day. Take a look back at your college experiences and write down what you see behind you. This is where you have to be creative. What did you do your first year in college that made your experience meaningful? What issues did you struggle with? How did you get over these issues? Who helped you to find the answers? Use your list of expectations to help guide you as you look back at the best college experience.

Naked Exercise #2

Patience, Patience, and More Patience

Forget giving it two weeks or two months! Give yourself at least a year or two to get comfortable with the uncomfortable on campus.

This is the part of the workbook where you will need to be patient. Patience is to expectations in college as gas is to a car's ability to drive—without enough of either you won't get where you want to go. (NOTE: I'm trying to get through the intro to this Naked Exercise as fast as possible; please be patient with me...this parenthetical aside took up too much time...I'm sorry...okay, I'll stop now...well, actually, now.)

I know, you want it all to happen right *now*. Impatient people are always flipping to the next page, focusing on why something isn't happening fast enough, and not listening. It's always about what's next. Impatient people will turn the page right now (Wait! Come back here!). They rarely stop and enjoy the moment.

STOP.

ENJOY THE MOMENT.

LOOK AROUND.

Using the academic, social, and emotional expectations you've listed in the previous exercise, identify what you expect to happen in college and how long you think it will take for these things to happen. Once you've compiled your list, factor in patience and thus add some time to your estimate, to recognize that things may not happen as quickly as you want them to. Then name the people who can help you get where you want, and who will help you get there faster.

While addressing what you want and when you want it, think about these questions:

1. Why am I in such a rush?

2. Could the experience be better if I were to factor in more time?

3. Might I be better prepared if I slowed down?

4. Could there be a negative side to getting it all too fast?

5. What might the long-term pay-off be if I factor in some patience?

What I want (based on expectations):

Find a girlfriend or boyfriend.

Time frame (how long it will take to get it):

By Friday night at 1 a.m. (technically Saturday morning).

Adjusted time frame + patience: .

By Sunday at noon.

Who can help me get there faster?

A desperate girl who is looking to find a boyfriend by Sunday morning.

* * *

What I want (based on expectations):

_____

Time frame (how long it will take to get it):

_____

Adjusted time frame + patience:

_____

Who can help me get there faster?

_____

* * *

What I want (based on expectations):

_____

Time frame (how long it will take to get it):

_____

Adjusted time frame + patience:

_____

Who can help me get there faster?

_____

* * *

What I want (based on expectations):

_____

Time frame (how long it will take to get it):

_____

Adjusted time frame + patience:

_____

Who can help me get there faster?

_____

* * *

What I want (based on expectations):

_____

Time frame (how long it will take to get it):

_____

Adjusted time frame + patience:

_____

Who can help me get there faster?

_____

✎ **Naked Journal #2:** The Naked Journey

The journey is the best part of the experience (well, one of the best parts). Think back to a journey you've taken in life when you were impatient or rushed into something. It could be speeding in your car, rushing into a relationship, rushing a play on the field, rushing a first kiss, or rushing to judgment. How could factoring in more patience have changed the outcome? How could you have thought about a situation differently to allow yourself to be more patient?

Naked Exercise #3

Finding Your Three Places on Campus

Your places are waiting for you. You just need to look for them and work to find them. Just know they are out there.

If you want to make friends, find a major, find a date, and have an amazing college experience, there's something you need to do...

Plan to work to find your places on campus.

One of the biggest mistakes new students make is thinking that everything will just happen automatically for them in college. Sure, it works this way for some students, but not for everyone. And a lot of people who find their places on campus quickly don't find the *right* place. It's easy to find the wrong place. This Naked Exercise will help you find the very best places.

People who do find their places quickly often know people on campus already, or they come to campus with a plan on how to find their place. But forget finding just ONE place—you're going to need to find THREE places. Why three places? You need to create a world of options. If you ever feel out of place, having at least three places always gives you somewhere to go. That's important.

Again, this won't happen in two weeks or even two months. It is something that can take time. But this will help you get comfortable with the uncomfortable. Patience pays off (see the previous exercise), so just remember, it takes time to find your place(s) in college.

NOTE TO HIGH SCHOOL STUDENTS: This is a great exercise to do *before* selecting your first-choice college. If you can figure out where you want to find your places, it will be easier to pick the right school for you.

Five Steps to Finding Three Places on Campus

Step 1
Identify activities, experiences, and hobbies that helped you find your place in high school.

Activity / Experience / Hobby:

_____

How this helped you find your place:

_____

* * *

Activity / Experience / Hobby:

_____

How this helped you find your place:

_____

* * *

Activity / Experience / Hobby:

_____

How this helped you find your place:

_____

Step 2

Identify activities, experiences, and hobbies that you want to do in college and why these are important to you. Pick at least one social, one academic, and one spiritual/ volunteer experience (turn to Naked Exercise #13 if you need help identifying clubs, activities, and organizations that interest you).

Activity/Organization:

_____

How this will help you find your place:

_____

* * *

Activity/Organization:

_____

How this will help you find your place:

_____

* * *

Activity/Organization:

_____

How this will help you find your place:

_____

Step 3

Identify people on campus who are already doing the things you want to do. How can you find these people? What step(s) can you take to get involved in each particular activity?

Activity/Organization:

_____

How to find people doing what you want to do:

_____

How you can get involved:

_____

* * *

Activity/Organization:

_____

How to find people doing what you want to do:

_____

How you can get involved:

_____

Activity/Organization:

_____

How to find people doing what you want to do:

_____

How you can get involved:

_____

Step 4

Contact the people doing the things you want to do and ask them how to get involved. If you're not comfortable contacting them, check out Naked Exercise #9—getting comfortable with the uncomfortable. This will help you finish step 4.

Activity/Organization:

_____

Contact name:

_____

Activity/Organization:

_____

Contact name:

_____

* * *

Activity/Organization:

_____

Contact name:

_____

Step 5

Get going! Remember, you are not supposed to know people on campus, so you can feel comfortable going to meetings, activities, and events on your own. Your job is to meet people so you can get to know more people. If you don't want to go at it on your own, consider inviting a friend to come along. This can be a roommate, someone down the hall, a friend from home, etc.

If you do go on your own, answer these questions:

- Why am I going to this meeting/event?
- Am I supposed to know people at the meeting/event?
- How can I get to know people at the meeting/event?
- How long will I give myself to get to know people?

If you don't want to go alone, put together a list of people you can ask to go with you.

1. _____

2. _____

3. _____

4. _____

5. _____

✎ **Naked Journal #3:** Naked Encounters

Think back to your most meaningful connections and experiences in high school. Identify one that jumps out at you. Share the story of how you found this meaningful connection and experience. How is it that you were able to establish this connection and have this experience? How did you meet the people you connected with? Who are the people who helped you to find this connection (parents, teachers, other friends, etc.)? How did you get involved in the activity or organization that changed your life (what steps did you take)? What were the greatest obstacles you faced? How were you able to overcome these obstacles? Can you do the same things in college? What would make it different in college?

Naked Exercise #4

When Lost or Confused, Ask for Help

Ready to get lost? Take this workbook to a place on campus where you've never been before. Do it during the day. Take a friend or classmate along. The goal here is to try to get lost on campus. (If you go to school in a place where there's a rough neighborhood or if you go to school in the woods, then you can just go somewhere that's safe and imagine that you're lost.)

Once you pick your spot, look for five people and ask for directions to get somewhere else on or near campus (pick a building, store, or restaurant).

Get in the habit of asking questions and approaching people for help. Here's where you'll record the results of your "Lost and Confused" expedition.

1. Where did you start and where did you want to go (specific addresses not

    necessary)? _____

2. How did people respond when you asked for help?

    Person #1: _____

    Person #2: _____

    Person #3: _____

Person #4: _____

Person #5: _____

3. How did it make you feel? _____

4. What surprised you? _____

5. Do you recommend this experiment? _____

Wherever you want to go on campus and in life, there are people who can help you get there. Whenever you have a question, reach out and ask for help. You will be surprised just how many people can (and are happy to) help you find directions.

(Feel free to use your college website or orientation booklet to help you answer these.)

Need academic help? Who are five people you can turn to?

Name: _____

Location (office): _____

Name: _____

Location (office): _____

Name: _____

Location (office): _____

Name: _____

Location (office): _____

Name: _____

Location (office): _____

* * *

Need mental health help? Who are five people you can turn to?

Name: _____

Location (office): _____

Name: _____

Location (office): _____

Name: _____

Location (office): _____

Name: _____

Location (office): _____

Name: _____

Location (office): _____

* * *

Need financial help? Who are five people you can turn to?

Name: _____

Location (office): _____

Name: _____

Location (office): _____

Name: _____

Location (office): _____

Name: _____

Location (office): _____

Name: _____

Location (office): _____

* * *

Need help dealing with a roommate? Who are five people you can turn to?

Name: _____

Location (office): _____

Name: _____

Location (office): _____

Name: _____

Location (office): _____

Name: _____

Location (office): _____

Name: _____

Location (office): _____

✎ Naked Journal #4: Lost and Found

Ever gotten lost while on a trip? Ever felt alone in life? Ever needed direction? Share a memory of a time when you felt lost, alone, and needed direction. How were you able to find your way? Who helped you find answers? What was the hardest part of the journey? What did you discover during this journey (about yourself or others)?

For a different perspective, also think about a time when *you* helped somebody. How did you feel when they asked you for help? What were your thoughts about them and their situation? How did it feel to be the one who could help? Does reflecting on your role in helping another change the way you think about asking another for help?

Naked Exercise #5

Be Yourself: Not Me, Not Him, Not Her

Being anyone else other than you can be exhausting. Once you start being someone else, you can't stop. The problem is that someone might discover the real you. Better to be yourself from the beginning and not have to keep pretending. It's far less exhausting.

So, who are you?

Really, who are you? (Me grabbing you by the shoulders and gently shaking you.)

Describe who you are in eleven words (or twelve if you need an extra one). Think about your very best qualities and list them below:

1. *Hotssssizzle*   5. _____   9. _____

2. _____   6. _____   10. _____

3. _____   7. _____   11. _____

4. _____   8. _____   12. _____

Describe who you want to become in college, in eleven words (twelve if you need them). You can use some of the same descriptive words from above. List the qualities that you want to exude and communicate to others.

1. *Confidence*   5. _____   9. _____

2. _____   6. _____   10. _____

3. _____   7. _____   11. _____

4. _____   8. _____   12. _____

Why is this important to you?

_____

_____

_____

Describe the kind of people you want to surround yourself with in college, in twelve words. (Why twelve? Okay, make it eleven...) (Examples: achievers, stoners, leaders, followers, etc.)

1. _Motivated_   5. _____   9. _____

2. _____   6. _____   10. _____

3. _____   7. _____   11. _____

4. _____   8. _____   12. _____

Where and how can you find these people?

_____

_____

_____

Another Promise to Yourself
Now, make this promise to yourself. This is important (don't skip).

I, _____, promise to give people on campus permission to think whatever they want about me. I will give them time to get to know me. When people misunderstand or judge me too quickly, I promise to remember my best qualities (on the previous page) and surround myself with other people who can get to know the authentic me.

Becoming the New College You
If you love who you are, then don't worry about changing. But if you want to make some changes, here's where it all begins. Part of starting a new life in college is having the opportunity to become anyone you want to become. As much as some of you might want to become someone else, recognizing and embracing who you were in the past can enable you to take incremental steps to become the person you want to be in the future. Take small steps from where you are today and over the next four years you'll become the person you hope to be.

What parts of the old high school YOU do you want to leave behind?

_____

_____

_____

How did you become the person you no longer want to be?

_____

_____

_____

Describe who you see yourself becoming in college. What will your life look like? What will you do in your free time? How will people look at you? How will you see yourself? What are you wearing?

_____

_____

_____

What is the biggest fear you have about taking the steps to become the new you?

_____

_____

_____

List three things you can do to overcome this fear (think about the people you can talk to on campus and the resources available).

1. _____

2. _____

3. _____

✎ Naked Journal #5: Naked Movies (No, Not Those Kind)

Think of your favorite teen movie—you know, the kind of movie where the main character is faced with moral and ethical dilemmas and comes out on top (*American Pie*, *Superbad*, etc.). Share the story of your favorite movie and how the story line in the movie applies to your college experience. How does this story translate into you creating a world in college where you can make the best choices to become the person you want to become?

Naked Exercise #6

About Your Parents...

They can be so loving and caring, but sometimes they can be too loving and caring. Are your parents bothering you? If so, it might not be their fault. It might have a lot to do with what you're doing with your cell phone, Facebook, and email.

If you didn't already know, parents are more involved in the college experience than ever before. It's way too easy for parents to be way too involved. If your mom or dad is reading this to you at this very second you know what I mean.

Do you know why they are so involved? Sure, part of it is their love for you and interest in your life. But a lot of the time they are so involved because you are the one texting, talking, emailing, chatting, and involving them, not to mention those frequent visits home. You are the one inviting them into all parts of your life.

This Naked Exercise is all about helping you to help your parents figure out how involved is involved just enough. And it's worth mentioning, I have a book for parents to help them make your life that much better: *The Naked Roommate: For Parents Only*.

Some Questions

What concerns you most about how your relationship will change with your parents once you begin living life in college?

_____

_____

_____

How do you think your parents are feeling about you leaving for college or attending college? Have you talked to them about their feelings?

_____

_____

_____

How often do you plan on communicating with your parents (this includes texting, calling, emailing, and chatting)?

_____ times a day / _____ days a week

Circle the days you plan on communicating with your parents.

MON / TUES / WED / THUR / FRI / SAT / SUN

Your preferred means of communication?

_____ Phone   _____ Email   _____ Texting   _____ Personal visit

Their preferred means of communication?

_____ Phone   _____ Email   _____ Texting   _____ Personal visit

How often do you think your parents will want to communicate with you?

_____

_____

_____

What will they want to know when they talk with you?

_____

_____

_____

Why do you think the things they'll want to talk about are important to them?

_____

_____

_____

Is this information you want to share? YES / NO
If not, why not?

_____

_____

_____

How might you explain this to them in a way that won't strain your relationship?

_____

_____

_____

How will you deal with difficult questions that you think cross the line?

_____

_____

_____

When is it appropriate to lie to your parents when sharing information?

_____

_____

_____

In what ways might you compromise so that both you and your parents feel a satisfactory level of communication?

_____

_____

_____

Do you expect your parents to solve your problems in college? YES / NO

Whether or not you want your parents to "fix" a problem, who are five people on campus who can help you find answers instead of your parents?

1. Problem: _____

    Contact on campus:_____

2. Problem: _____

    Contact on campus:_____

3. Problem: _____

    Contact on campus:_____

4. Problem: _____

    Contact on campus:_____

5. Problem: _____

    Contact on campus:_____

Parents and Facebook

Will you allow your parents to be your Facebook friend? YES / NO
If NO, why not?

_____

_____

_____

Explain your answer here:

_____

_____

_____

If your parents want to be your Facebook friend and you do not want them to be your friend, what can you do to compromise?

_____

_____

_____

Setting Parental Limits

- Will you want them to call your professors if you're having problems?

  YES / NO

- Will you want them to call your roommate and ask questions about you?

  YES / NO

- If living away from home, will you want your parents to visit without asking?

  YES / NO

- Will you want your parents to call the residence life staff to resolve conflicts?

YES / NO

- Will you want your parents to have access to your grades?

YES / NO

- Will you want your parents to have access to your medical records?

YES / NO

- When you call your parents, do you want advice or do you want someone to fix everything?

YES / NO

What do you plan on doing to solve your own problems instead of relying on your parents to help you navigate through conflict, crisis, or confusion?

_____

_____

_____

It is up to you to build the right relationship with your parents during your college years. Discuss limits. Talk about expectations. Have open dialogue. Give your parents permission to not always see the world how you see it. Give yourself permission to make choices that aren't the same choices they would like you to make (but when you do, make sure the choice you do make is in fact the best choice).

✎ Naked Journal #6: The Thank-You Note

Want to surprise and shock your parents? Write your mom or dad a thank-you note (and don't ask for money in it). Just take a second and thank them. (You can always text them for money later.) If you only have a relationship with one parent, that works too. If a grandparent has filled the role of parent, that works too.

You can write your own letter or you can use this letter.

Sample letter:

Dear [insert Mom or Dad],

I just wanted to thank you for everything you've done for me over the years. You can trust that everything you've taught me will help guide me throughout my years in college. Do not worry—I will do everything you expect me to do. And if I don't do it, you won't know so just assume I'm being responsible. I love you. I know you're expecting me to ask you for money, but this isn't a letter asking for anything other than the time it took for me to tell you thank you and I love you.

Signed,

Your son or daughter

Naked Exercise #7

Homesickness: Breathe Deep, It's in the Air

Homesickness on campus is a lot like herpes on campus—a lot of people are secretly dealing with it, but few people are talking about it (although more people get homesick than herpes). About one in five students will get herpes. Can you guess how many will get homesick? That's right...did someone say NAKED TRIVIA TIME? Wahoooooo!

Naked Trivia
What percentage of students admit feeling some sort of homesickness?

    a. 20.1 percent

    b. 32.1 percent

    c. 45.1 percent

    d. 60 percent

The answer is...the answer is the letter that comes after "C" and before "E" in the alphabet (I don't want to write it just in case someone is looking at this while answering the question). That's right, nearly two-thirds get homesick.

You might just get homesick. It might not happen today or tomorrow, but there's a good chance it will happen at some point. When it does, remind yourself that it's normal, natural, and expected. The cure is to be patient, reach out for help, and work to make your new campus a home that you will be sick to leave four, five, or six years from now. It will get better. Remember, the cure for homesickness is not at home.

Things Making You Homesick

Check the following that apply to you:

_____ I feel like everyone is having a better time than me.

_____ Sometimes I just feel like crying.

_____ I feel alone even when I'm with my roommate(s).

_____ I feel alone when surrounded by friends.

_____ I'm afraid my friends from high school will forget about me.

_____ I feel lost and out of sorts on a regular basis.

_____ I miss my room and my things.

_____ I miss my parents.

_____ I miss my close friends from home.

_____ I miss my pet at home.

_____ I thought I would make friends faster.

_____ I thought I would feel happier here.

_____ I don't feel like myself.

_____ I'm always second-guessing myself.

_____ I can't relax and I often feel on edge.

_____ Little things stress me out.

_____I have a hard time concentrating in class.

_____ I feel out of control.

_____ I'm having trouble finding people I can feel close too.

_____ I want to go home.

For each item you checked, identify at least one action you can take on campus to try to turn your new home into a more comfortable home. For example, if you checked that you're feeling stressed, make an appointment with a counselor on campus, take a yoga class, or remind yourself that it takes time to find your place. If you miss your pet, see about getting a fish if it's allowed. Find out if there is an animal shelter or pet store nearby where you could do some volunteer work. Get creative. It's easy to go home when you feel homesick, but the solution isn't at home. It's in your ability to make a home on campus.

Checked Item	What Would Help Me Feel Better (at College)
1. _____	_____
2. _____	_____
3. _____	_____
4. _____	_____
5. _____	_____
6. _____	_____
7. _____	_____

For those of you *not* feeling homesick, what advice would you give to those who are feeling homesick? What steps have you taken to help yourself feel connected to campus and the people around you?

_____

_____

The Love List

When stuck in a homesickness haze, it's extremely hard to see the good parts of college life. They are there. You just need to take a step back (if seated, just scoot back in your chair instead of stepping back), and take a moment to think about all the good things at college. What would you miss if you left school?

Here is a list to get you started:

_____ Keeping my own hours

_____ Coming and going as I please

_____ Not having a curfew

_____ Making the decision to go to class (or not)

_____ Determining how much schoolwork I do and when

_____ Spending time with whomever I choose

_____ Doing what I want with whomever I want

_____ Deciding when, where, and what I eat

Now it's your turn. Make a list of the things you like or love about college. They don't have to make you super happy; they can just be the perks of living away from home. Think of these as things you'd miss if you weren't at school.

_____

_____

_____

Keep this list close to you. When you are feeling down and thinking about running home, remind yourself of the things you like about this place. Remember, it takes time to find your place on campus. Look into the future and avoid living in the past.

✎ Naked Journal #7: The Cure for Homesickness

Talk to at least three upperclassmen (juniors and seniors) and ask about their greatest homesick moment. (They will have one, and if they say they don't, they're probably not being truthful.) Ask what they missed about home the most. How long did the homesickness last? And what did they do to get over the homesickness? Ask what advice they would give to new students to help them get over the feeling of homesickness. Write the answers in a short journal entry.

NOTE: Do not reveal your sources' names in the journal (although keep a note somewhere of who they are if your instructor needs verification).

Naked Exercise #8

Technology: The Fifth Wall

If you're texting while on the phone while chatting via your webcam while reading this tip, you might be stuck behind the fifth wall of technology (and be very talented!). The Internet, cell phones, IM, video games, and electronic devices you plug in or charge create what is known as the fifth wall of technology. Physically you might be on campus, but mentally and emotionally you're somewhere else.

This is an important Naked Exercise (not to diminish the importance of all the other exercises)! College can be an amazing experience, but it can also be socially uncomfortable at times. Remember the 10 percent BS? When it arrives, it's all too easy to run and hide in your comfort zone by using technology. I'm talking about things like calling home, texting old friends, hanging out on Facebook, surfing the Internet, and playing video games online with random people OTHER than people on campus.

Check all that apply and estimate (honestly) how much time on average you spend a day doing these things (your best guess).

Technology	Hours per Day
_____ Talking on your cell phone with friends from home	_____
_____ Texting friends from home	_____
_____ Instant Messaging friends from home	_____
_____ Hanging out in chat rooms or playing games	_____
_____ Surfing the Web	_____
_____ Downloading music	_____
_____ Watching videos on your phone or other device	_____
_____ Watching TV	_____
_____ Hanging out on Facebook	_____
_____ Tweeting	_____
_____ Listening to music	_____
_____ Playing video games	_____
Daily total:	_____

Multiply this number by seven and you get the total for the week. (Whoa! That's a big number.) Multiply it by 30 and get your total for the month. Multiply it by 365 and...oh my that's an insanely large number! Can you believe you've spent that much time not talking to people face to face?

Here's the Math

Let's just say hypothetically you spend 3 hours talking on the phone a day, 1 hour texting a day, 1 hour gaming a day, 1 hour of TV, and 1 hour of Facebook, that equals 7 hours a day, 28 hours a week, 1,456 hours a year. That's over 60 days stuck behind the fifth wall of technology. And you wonder why some people don't feel connected to life on campus...(or are single).

The Big Question

Is the majority of your time spent online connecting with old friends from home rather than helping you make new friends on campus? YES / NO

If yes, how do you think spending so much time communicating with people you already know (and who are no longer part of your daily life) impacts meeting new people on campus (yes, a loaded question)?

_____

_____

_____

What steps can you take to use technology to communicate LESS with people from home and MORE with people on campus?

_____

_____

_____

If friends, family, or significant others at home insist on pulling you back behind the fifth wall of technology, what can you say or do to set limits?

_____

_____

_____

Social Networking No-Nos

Just in case you didn't know, you can get expelled, lose a job, or miss out on a leadership position based on your social networking resume. Everything you say, write, and post online can be accessed by the world. It's forever. Even if you set restrictions on who can read your posts, there are ways they can still get out—fake friends, jealous exes, or strangers can share your information with the world (or TMZ). Make sure you answer NO to all the social media no-nos.

- There are pictures of me consuming alcohol while underage online.

YES / NO

- People can gain access to my cell phone and address through Facebook.

YES / NO

- There are pictures of me doing something illegal online.

YES / NO

- There are pictures of me doing something that a professor, employer, or someone I respect might consider to be in poor taste.

YES / NO

- People have posted incriminating info on my wall.

YES / NO

- I accept friend requests from anyone who requests me.

YES / NO

- I don't have privacy settings in place.

YES / NO

- I post blog entries that share my personal information.

YES / NO

- I've posted hateful messages.

YES / NO

- There may be pictures of me with other people doing something illegal.

YES / NO

- I change my password once a month.

YES / NO

What is the worst story you've ever heard about social networking gone bad?

_____

_____

_____

List ten Internet safety concerns most students don't think about when texting, Facebooking, and using social networks.

1. _____

2. _____

3. _____

4. _____

5. _____

6. _____

7. _____

8. _____

9. _____

10. _____

* * *

True or False

And now some VERY difficult true or false questions about how you use technology to finish this Naked Exercise:

1. Texting in class is considered polite and respectful.

    True or False

2. Taking and texting naked pictures of yourself is a GREAT idea.

    True or False

3. It's a good idea to accept anyone's Facebook friendship request.

    True or False

4. Facebook privacy settings will keep all of your information private from future scandal.

    True or False

5. Posting your cell phone number will allow everyone who wants to harass you an opportunity to call and text you.

    True or False

6. Everything you write, post, email, and say on social networking sites is available for the world to consume.

    True or False

✎ Naked Journal #8: The Headline Culture

Ever posted a status update that didn't share the whole truth? Ever read a status update and think that everyone is having a better time than you?

We all make assumptions based on headlines and updates. Sometimes just looking at people's posts can make it seem like everyone is having a better time than you are. But remember that when people send out these posts or statuses, they're not telling you the whole story.

For this naked journal, post ten status updates that make the world think life is good. Then post the status updates that don't make it out into the news feed.

Example:

Status Update: *Harlan went on the best date of his life.*

Status Update NOT Broadcasted: *Two days later the girl never called him back.*

Status Update: *Harlan is at the best party of his life.*

Status Update NOT Broadcasted: *Harlan's friend was rushed to the hospital because he drank so much that he passed out.*

Naked Exercise #9

The Risk-Taking Project

Life in college is about taking risks. And living a life driven by passion means taking risks. When I mention risk-taking in this section, I'm not talking about jumping out of an airplane or skiing down the roof of your house (yes, you can look that video up on YouTube). I'm talking about emotional risks, academic risks, social risks, and sometimes even physical risks. I'm talking actions like approaching new people, making friends, sitting at a table with people you don't know, getting help from an unfamiliar professor, finding a date (while sober—even riskier), talking in front of the class, saying NO to someone pressuring you to do something that doesn't feel right—these are the kinds of risks that are part of living life in college. Facing these kinds of challenges can be uncomfortable at times. But managing these social, emotional, and academic risks is an essential part of finding your place on campus, making new friends, and having a meaningful college experience. It will prepare you for a life of personal growth and change.

And with that, it's time for a NAKED Questionnaire!

Part 1. Comfort Zone Questionnaire

For each of the following items, identify how comfortable or uncomfortable each action makes you feel by circling a value using the following rating scale:

	VERY Comfortable (Easy Risk) ⟶	VERY Uncomfortable (Very Difficult Risk)
	1 2 3 4 5 6 7 8 9 10	

1. Sitting at a table and eating a meal with people you don't know

   1 2 3 4 5 6 7 8 9 10

2. Asking a question in class about something you don't understand, in front of the entire class

   1 2 3 4 5 6 7 8 9 10

3. Attending school away from home

   1 2 3 4 5 6 7 8 9 10

4. Talking with your professors one-on-one during office hours

   1 2 3 4 5 6 7 8 9 10

5. Not talking to or texting your parents on a daily basis

   1 2 3 4 5 6 7 8 9 10

6. Voicing an opinion different from that of the group

   1 2 3 4 5 6 7 8 9 10

7. Running for an elected office

   1 2 3 4 5 6 7 8 9 10

8. Volunteering for a cause you believe in

   1 2 3 4 5 6 7 8 9 10

9. Seeking academic help from a campus resource

   1 2 3 4 5 6 7 8 9 10

10. Telling a friend that you are interested in "more"

    1 2 3 4 5 6 7 8 9 10

11. Asking someone you don't know on a date

    1 2 3 4 5 6 7 8 9 10

12. Dating someone from a different racial, religious, or cultural background

    1 2 3 4 5 6 7 8 9 10

13. Speaking in front of a large group

    1 2 3 4 5 6 7 8 9 10

	VERY Comfortable (Easy Risk)					VERY Uncomfortable (Very Difficult Risk)				
	1	2	3	4	5	6	7	8	9	10
14. Avoiding consumption of alcohol at gatherings where most of the people around you are drinking	1	2	3	4	5	6	7	8	9	10
15. Turning down an invitation to a social event in order to study or write a paper	1	2	3	4	5	6	7	8	9	10
16. Applying for a highly competitive internship, graduate program, or job	1	2	3	4	5	6	7	8	9	10
17. Performing your talent in front of an audience	1	2	3	4	5	6	7	8	9	10
18. Taking part in a team sport competition	1	2	3	4	5	6	7	8	9	10
19. Changing your physical appearance (style of dress, hairstyle, wearing/not wearing makeup, getting a tattoo or piercing)	1	2	3	4	5	6	7	8	9	10
20. Telling a friend how you honestly feel, knowing that he or she may get defensive, hurt, or angry	1	2	3	4	5	6	7	8	9	10
21. Traveling abroad by yourself	1	2	3	4	5	6	7	8	9	10
22. Exploring a new religion (other than your current one)	1	2	3	4	5	6	7	8	9	10
23. Changing your major	1	2	3	4	5	6	7	8	9	10
24. Choosing a major your parents do not support	1	2	3	4	5	6	7	8	9	10

	VERY Comfortable (Easy Risk) ⟶				VERY Uncomfortable (Very Difficult Risk)				
	1	2	3	4	5	6	7	8	9	10

25. Attending a club/organization meeting in which you don't know any of the members
1 2 3 4 5 6 7 8 9 10

26. Telling someone that you need personal help due to worry, stress, homesickness, anxiety, or depression
1 2 3 4 5 6 7 8 9 10

27. Breaking up with a boyfriend or girlfriend
1 2 3 4 5 6 7 8 9 10

28. Going out to dinner or a movie by yourself
1 2 3 4 5 6 7 8 9 10

29. Forming a friendship with someone of a different sexual orientation than yours
1 2 3 4 5 6 7 8 9 10

30. Doing something that you know will make you happier, but will likely upset the people closest to you
1 2 3 4 5 6 7 8 9 10

Part 2. Assessing Your Results

1. Review the items from the "Comfort Zone Questionnaire." List all the actions that ranked a value of 5 or lower. These are areas where you feel confident and comfortable:

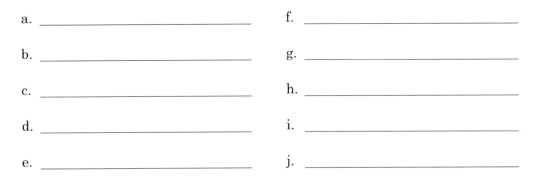

a. _____   f. _____

b. _____   g. _____

c. _____   h. _____

d. _____   i. _____

e. _____   j. _____

2. Now list all the actions that ranked a value of 6 or higher. These are areas where you feel uneasy and uncomfortable:

a. _____   f. _____

b. _____   g. _____

c. _____   h. _____

d. _____   i. _____

e. _____   j. _____

3. How have you been limited by your narrow comfort zone in these particular areas? What haven't you experienced or accomplished because taking the risk made you uncomfortable? What have you missed out on?

_____

_____

_____

4. Describe some specific ways in which you could benefit if you were to overcome what limits you in these areas.

_____

_____

_____

5. Based on your previous response, identify three "risks" that you would like to take this year in order to work to get comfortable with the uncomfortable and expand your comfort zone.

a. _____

b. _____

c. _____

Part 3. Preparing for the Risk

NAKED NOTE: There are two more worksheets in the back of the workbook that include Parts 3 and 4 so you can repeat this exercise.

1. Define one risk you're going to take
Explain the risk you will take and your plan of action for taking this risk.

_____

_____

_____

2. Possible obstacles
List three potential obstacles standing in the path to achieving your desired outcome.

1. _____

2. _____

3. _____

3. Preparing for obstacles
From the list of potential obstacles, list one action that you will take to help overcome each anticipated obstacle. Use the resources, support services, and people on and off campus to help you prepare for your risk.

1. _____

2. _____

3. _____

4. People in your corner

Who are the people whom you can enlist to support you, guide you, and help you navigate through this particular risk (think of a boxer who enters the ring and the people in the boxer's corner helping him or her win)?

1. _____   4. _____

2. _____   5. _____

3. _____   6. _____

5. Expectations

Write a one-paragraph summary of your desired outcome for this particular risk.

_____

_____

_____

_____

_____

_____

Some Encouragement before Taking the Risk

As someone who is rooting for you and in your corner, I want to make sure you approach this risk while keeping a few things in mind.

1. Embrace the Universal Rejection Truth of taking risks. In other words, give the world permission to respond however the world will respond. Some risks will go as planned, but not all. Embrace the experience and the outcome will always be favorable.

2. Should your risk turn out as planned—FANTASTIC. Should it not turn out as planned—FANTASTIC. Taking risks and navigating through your outcome, favorable or not, is a victory. That said, working through the undesired outcomes will ultimately enable you to achieve the outcomes you desire.

3. REMEMBER—this is an experiment. Try not to get emotional. If this project is too hard physically or emotionally, enlist the help of professional therapists and counselors on campus. This exercise is about living a life driven by passion. It can get intense at times.

1, 2, 3

TAKE YOUR RISK

A Few Tips while Taking Your Risk:

1. The challenge or risk you take on should have received approval by your instructor (if you're in a class) as something appropriate for the scope and spirit of this assignment.

2. Your activity should *not* endanger you or another person in any way. This is not a challenge about putting yourself in harm's way or engaging in a physical activity that is "risky" in the sense that it is illegal, violates the Student Code of Conduct, or could cause property damage, illness, or injury. It's an emotional or social risk.

3. Your risk should be something that will help you get over a personal, academic, or social obstacle. Take your risk and watch your world change!

Part 4. The Risk-Taking Results

This is where you get to share what happened. Remember, just having taken this risk is a HUGE success. Celebrate! You did it!

1. Outcome of your risk
Explain how the risk unfolded in detail.

---

2. Your reaction to the results
Explain your feelings and how you reacted before, during, and after the risk.

_____

_____

_____

3. Evaluating the results
Did you achieve your desired outcome?

_____

Did your risk-taking go as planned or not as planned?

_____

_____

Why didn't it go as planned? Why did it go as planned?

_____

_____

What advice or guidance did you receive from the people in your corner?

_____

_____

_____

Was this advice and guidance helpful? If so, how? If not, why not?

_____

_____

_____

What surprised you the most about your risk-taking experience?

_____

_____

_____

What did you learn from this experience?

_____

_____

_____

If you take this risk again, what will you do differently the next time?

_____

_____

_____

✎ Naked Journal #9: The Risk-Taking Results

Now it's time to fill out the paperwork. For this entry, you should think of yourself as a participant in the International Risk-Taking Project. Or think of this journal as a conversation on paper.

This is the *story* of your risk-taking experience. The worksheet on the previous pages should help you organize your thoughts and make this an easy conversation.

Your conversation on paper should include (but not necessarily in this order) the following:

1. Summarize the experiment.

   a. Describe the risk you took.

   b. How does it reflect a change you would like to make in your life?

   c. Why is this change important to you?

   d. How did you see this particular risk as enabling you to start making a change in this area of importance?

   e. What made it a "risk" to you?

   f. What kind of support or guidance did you receive from people in your corner?

   g. How much did the support of others help you during this process?

2. Explain in detail the outcome of your risk.

   a. Was it what you had hoped for? Why or why not?

   b. Why did it go as planned? Why did it not go as planned?

3. Explain in detail your reaction to the results in relation to what you hoped it would accomplish.

   a. What surprised you the most about your risk-taking experience?

   b. If you take this risk again, what will you do differently next time?

   c. What did you ultimately learn from this experience?

P.S. I'd love to read your paper. I might even be able to include it in future book projects. Please send a copy to: Harlan@HelpMeHarlan.com (subject: Risk-Taking Final Paper).

Want More Nakedness?

Website: www.NakedRoommate.com
Facebook: www.Facebook.com/TNRFanPage
Twitter: @NakedRoommate

Designated Doodling Space

Rate using a scale of 1–10.

> **1 = Not true → 5 = Somewhat true → 10 = Doesn't get any truer**

_____ I have a good idea of how I'll make friends.

_____ I plan to pursue the same activities I participated in when I was in high school.

_____ I don't want to attend a club meeting or campus event by myself.

_____ I'm looking forward to branching out, meeting new people, and discovering new things about myself.

_____ I'm attending college with friends from high school.

_____ I'm worried that when I see my old high school friends, everything will be different and that will be hard for me.

_____ I have attended several events on campus.

_____ I plan on getting involved in activities and organizations my first year in college.

_____ I don't want to have anything to do with the people I went to high school with—I am glad to leave it all behind.

_____ Most of the people I've met in college so far are not my "type."

_____ I will probably transfer to a different school eventually.

_____ I already know of at least a few groups on campus that I want to get involved in.

_____ I am looking forward to trying out the new "college me" on the new people I meet in classes and clubs on campus.

Naked Exercise #10

Shopping for Friends

Most students come to college hungry to make friends. Everyone is in the market. But unless you are accessible and available for people to meet you, these friendly friend-seeking people will be forced to shop somewhere else for friends.

How do I make new friends? Where do I make new friends? How long will it take for me to make new friends? Will these be good friends? Will I be able to handle missing my friends from home?

These are some of the most common questions new students have. They are all good questions, with answers that will unfold in the coming months and years.

Understand that most new students come to campus looking for friends. Even people who appear to already have friends are interested in finding new friends. There are *always* people looking for friends. While the first few weeks feel like prime friend-making time, they aren't the only time to connect with potential friends. In fact, the best friendships grow over time. The problem is that too many students get impatient or don't get involved enough to meet the people who can become great friends.

Here's the formula for making friends:

Shared experiences + time = new friendships

For the first time in your life you may be the one to have to make an effort to make new friends. Friends might not just come to you. If you are lucky enough to be involved in a sport or a group where shared experiences are part of your daily life, you'll make friends. But still, you need more than one group of friends.

Think about your past friendships from high school and how you connected with people in the past. This should help you figure out how to make friends in college. Team sports, clubs, and classes are just a few ways it happens.

Your Closest Friends from High School

Friend #1 _____

Friend #2 _____

Friend #3 _____

How did you meet your closest friends?

#1 _____

_____

#2 _____

_____

#3 _____

_____

How long did it take to form the friendships?

#1 _____

_____

#2 _____

_____

#3 _____

_____

What activities/events helped you form close friendships?

#1 _____

_____

#2 _____

_____

#3 _____

_____

Did anything surprise you about how you made friends?

_____

_____

_____

The Formula for Making Friends

Shared Experiences + Time = New Friendships

If you hide in your room, the library, online, or off campus and avoid getting involved, you will avoid having shared experiences. If you make the decision to get involved and engage in shared experiences over a long period of time, you can count on making new friends. Never forget that making trusted friends takes time.

So, how are you going to make these friends? Think about the kinds of experiences you want to share with others on campus. Browse the campus website for clubs, activities, and organizations that match your interests (or inspire new ones). List all of those that you might like to check out.

Campus clubs or organizations that I plan to get more information about:

1. _____

2. _____

3. _____

4. _____

5. _____

6. _____

7. _____

8. _____

9. _____

10. _____

How much time will you give yourself to form meaningful friendships?

_____ Weeks

_____ Months

_____ Years

✎ **Naked Journal #10:** Friendly Research

For this journal entry you'll need to talk to some juniors, seniors, and super-seniors on campus. Approach at least two, and try to find those who came to campus not knowing many (or any) people. Ask them how they met or were introduced to their friends, and how they've been able to meet people on campus. Reflect on their answers and describe how it inspires you to enhance your social life.

Naked Exercise #11

Temporary Friends vs. Full-Time Friends

Some friendships will last a lifetime; other friendships will last a few days or hours (although the memory of a bad friendship might last a lifetime). These are the friendly facts about making friends in college.

The Friendly Truth

Anyone can find "friends" in college. The challenge is finding the right kinds of friends. By that I mean friends you genuinely like to hang out with. The kinds of friends whom you respect and who respect you. The opposite of friends you can't stand to be around (and yes, you know those types of friends).

Finding the right kinds of friends means finding friends with common interests. For example, if you're someone who doesn't drink or do drugs, people who love to drink and do drugs would be the wrong type of friends. The challenge is that everyone needs friends in life, and sometimes, not knowing people on campus can mean making the wrong kinds of friends out of desperation. So make sure you take time to be discriminating with whom you choose to share your time with.

Qualities you value and want to find in a friend:

1. _____

2. _____

3. _____

4. _____

5. _____

Qualities that do not appeal to you in a friend:

1. _____

2. _____

3. _____

4. _____

5. _____

Qualities you will not tolerate and will cause you to forgo someone as a friend:

1. _____

2. _____

3. _____

4. _____

5. _____

Think about the new people you have met so far in college. Do they meet your standards for a friend? Are these people you want to hang out with on a regular basis? Without naming names, what bothers you about a friend or two, if anything?

_____

_____

_____

You don't need to end these relationships completely, but you should *definitely* make an effort to meet other people that are a better fit for you and have greater potential to become friends.

Where can you find friends who match your criteria? Think about five places on campus where people with similar interests hang out (you can always go back and fill this in once you finish the naked activities and organization section).

1. _____

2. _____

3. _____

4. _____

5. _____

If you find yourself having a hard time finding temporary or permanent friends, that's not unusual. It takes time to form meaningful, close relationships—even with people who share a lot in common with you. In the meantime, keep checking out activities around campus that provide opportunities to get to know people (at the very least, it will keep you busy).

Spiritual organizations and student organizations are great places to take on leadership roles. This way you don't have to worry about being invited to events—no one needs to invite you when it's your job to run an event.

Five ways to pass the time while making close friends:

1. _____

2. _____

3. _____

4. _____

5. _____

✎ Naked Journal #11: Naked Friends

What kind of friend are you? Why would someone be lucky to be your friend? What are all *your* BEST friend qualities? Write a description of the type of friend you are and the type of friend you've been. Use this to ALWAYS remember just how lucky people will be to meet you and be your friend. It's easy to forget while in the friendship gap (that's the time between having close friends in high school and good friends in college). Never forget who you are and what you have to offer, and people will learn. Sometimes it takes time—and the right people to notice.

Naked Exercise #12

Getting Involved: What, Where, When, How, and Why (but Not in That Order)

The sooner you can get involved, the faster you'll start feeling connected to the people and places on campus that will make life in college the very BEST experience.

Everyone says, "Get involved!" That's the number-one piece of advice students offered up in *The Naked Roommate* when I asked the question, "What's the number-one piece of advice you would offer students?"

You ask, "Why is it so important to get involved?" Great question! Thanks for asking! I've included some of the top reasons. See if you can think of some more.

Getting involved can help me to...

1. make friends

2. meet professors

3. build a professional resume

4. find a date

5. find a job

6. hook up

7. discover my interests

8. travel and see the world

9. de-stress

10. stay active

11. _____

12. _____

13. _____

14. _____

15. _____

16. _____

17. _____

18. _____

19. _____

20. _____

Clearly, it's important to get involved on campus. So if it's something that everyone should do and there are so many reasons to get involved, why is it that not everyone does it? What happens?

What are some reasons why you (or others) don't get involved?

1. _____

2. _____

3. _____

4. _____

5. _____

For all the reasons you've listed in the previous answer, can there still be ways you can get involved and manage life on campus?

For example, if you can't get involved because you have to work, can you get a job on campus that can help you make money, work on campus, and meet people? Could you try to get a scholarship and help free up time so that you can get involved? If you don't have enough time because you're focusing on your studies, is there a way you can use your studies to get involved? How about getting involved in an academic organization?

For each reason you listed, identify a way (or ways!) you can still get involved.

_____

_____

_____

_____

_____

_____

Getting involved is how you find your place inside and outside the classroom. It's the richest part of the college experience. It's what can help determine your success and pave a path to your future. Don't just get involved in things or the things your friends are doing. Always remember to create a world of options. The more options you have, the more people you'll meet.

BUT getting involved isn't as easy as just wanting to get involved. There's a big obstacle. Know what it is?

C'mon, just take a guess...

Your guess here:

_____

_____

_____

The answer is: The biggest obstacle is you.

The challenge is that getting involved sometimes means having to put yourself in uncomfortable and new situations. It can mean walking into rooms where you don't know people and sitting next to and talking to people who don't know you. This can cause you to feel like you are being judged or are being annoying. And new students in a new place don't like being judged or annoying.

So, how do you go it alone and not feel like a loser? How can you get involved and overcome a fear of looking bad or being judged by people you don't know? Answering these questions should help...

1. What do you find most intimidating about meeting new people?

_____

_____

_____

2. Do you think you should already know people in the clubs, activities, and organizations that interest you? YES / NO

3. Are you someone worth getting to know? YES / NO

4. How do you think other people will get to know you?

_____

_____

_____

Here are some things to think about regarding your answers.

YES, you are someone worth getting to know (if it's NO then head to the health center and meet with a therapist). And NO, you are NOT supposed to already know people in clubs, activities, and organizations.

As for how others will get to know you—they'll need to overcome their inhibitions and concerns that you will judge them negatively and find the courage to approach you (did you realize that they may be nervous to make *your* acquaintance?).

So, if you are someone worth knowing, and you aren't supposed to know people already, why does participating in an activity where you don't know people and aren't supposed to know people feel like such a problem?

It's all in how you view the situation. So how can you reframe getting involved so that you don't feel so uncomfortable when flying solo? I'll help you out with a couple of examples:

1. I'm not going to an event alone. I'm meeting someone. I just don't know who I'm meeting because the people I'm meeting are people I don't know yet.

2. There will be other people going alone. Therefore, I won't be alone in going alone. In fact, I'm helping the other people who are going alone.

3. <u>I can bring a notebook and make it an assignment. I can make it part of my Risk-</u>

    <u>Taking Project (see Naked Exercise #9). Even if it's not an assignment, I can write</u>

    <u>it up and use it as extra credit.</u>

4. _____

    _____

    _____

5. _____

    _____

    _____

6. _____

    _____

    _____

7. _____

    _____

    _____

If You Don't Want to Go Alone

I know there are still some of you who don't go to events on your own. If this is you, one way to make doing new things more comfortable is to reach out ahead of time to the executive board members and leaders of a group or organization and ask questions. This will give you a chance to have a relationship with people involved in the organization or activity *before* attending a meeting. Once at the event, you will already have someone you have talked to and therefore "know" a little. Then they can introduce you to other people.

Another thing you can do is invite people you kind of know, but want to get know better. Most people are just waiting for someone to do something and have someone to go with. Make your plans here:

Club, organization, or event: _____

Who I can contact before attending event: _____

People I can invite to go with me: _____

* * *

Club, organization, or event: _____

Who I can contact before attending event: _____

People I can invite to go with me: _____

* * *

Club, organization, or event: _____

Who I can contact before attending event: _____

People I can invite to go with me: _____

✎ Naked Journal #12: An "Involved" Journal Entry

The best way to discover how to get involved is to talk to the people who are involved. For this journal entry, your assignment is to contact a member of a club or organization who holds a leadership position in the group. This can be the president, vice president, treasurer, secretary, or a board member. Find out how this person got involved in the group, why this person got involved, and his or her BEST experience and WORST experience in the club or organization. Find out how getting involved impacted this person's life. Who knows, this little interview might just be your inspiration for getting involved yourself.

Naked Exercise #13

Clubs and Organizations:
A Smorgasbord of Opportunities

There's an all-you-can-do buffet of opportunities awaiting you. Don't just go for one dish. Fill your plate! And then go back for seconds, thirds, and fourths (note: be careful of the freshman 15).

Naked Student Involvement

What's the best way to find your place on campus and have the most amazing experiences? The answer is easy...GET INVOLVED! The opposite would be NOT getting involved. Don't do that. It will ensure that you will meet very few people and have no life other than the one that accidentally happens to you. When you do get involved, don't just get involved in one club, activity, or organization. Get involved in a few. If you get involved in several groups, you'll find that you live in a world of options. Having options means meeting different types of people with different interests—how interesting. When looking into campus clubs, activities, and organizations, try to identify one social event or organization, one academic event or organization, and one spiritual event or organization. Fill out the following information to help you get involved.

1. Social Activities and Organizations

Social activities and organizations include athletics, Greek life, peer education, volunteer groups, political activism, student organizations, clubs, athletics, special interest groups, and pretty much anything that interests you (note: some of these might fall into the spiritual organization category too, but that's okay). The activities and organizations should all be officially recognized by your school. All officially recognized activities and organizations will have faculty or staff advisors and be listed on the campus website. Browse the website, and visit the dean of students office or student activities office to make sure you have a complete list of currently active groups. Talk to residence life staff, contact a teaching assistant, post a note on Facebook, and identify fifteen social activities or organizations that interest you.

Fifteen campus clubs or organizations that look interesting to me:

1. _____   9. _____

2. _____   10. _____

3. _____   11. _____

4. _____   12. _____

5. _____   13. _____

6. _____   14. _____

7. _____   15. _____

8. _____

The three that really, really interest me:

1. _____

2. _____

3. _____

And the winner is (my most favorite at this point):

1. _____

Essential details and info:

Where it meets: _____

When it meets: _____

How you get involved: _____

Potential time commitment: _____

Advisor's name: _____

President's info: _____

Names and contact info of other officers: _____

_____

Who to contact for more info: _____

Your plan for getting involved: _____

_____

How long you will give this before deciding if you like the activity or event (one

meeting or event is NEVER enough): _____

2. Academic Activities and Organizations

Academic organizations are an easy place to find connections, improve grades, and make amazing contacts (including faculty). Don't be misled—they are not just about doing academic things and sitting around thinking or doing additional studying. Sometimes these organizations are actually more social in nature. They may exist to connect you with peers, faculty, and professionals in the discipline (and often sponsor events with free food!). They may provide opportunities to connect with the community at large (and companies in that community) through service projects and other volunteering events where you get to meet and greet people who could play an important role in your future.

Consider your major and what you would like to be when you grow up. What kinds of things would you like to do now? What experiences would be important to have in order to build your skills in your area, and what activities could you participate in that would increase your knowledge to make you more competitive at graduation time? For example, if you are a biology major, would you like to work in a lab and look at things under an electron microscope? If you are an accounting major, would you like to get a feel for doing the books for a large company and what tax issues they must account for? If you want to be a teacher, wouldn't you like to step into a real classroom and see what it is like to inspire a group of students?

Five academic activities or organizations that might interest me:

1. _____   4. _____

2. _____   5. _____

3. _____

These three really seem appealing:

1. _____

2. _____

3. _____

And the winner is (my most favorite at this point):

1. _____

Essential details and info:

Where it meets: _____

When it meets: _____

How you get involved: _____

Potential time commitment: _____

Advisor's name: _____

President's info: _____

Names and contact info of other officers: _____

_____

Who to contact for more info: _____

Your plan for getting involved: _____

_____

How long you will give this before deciding if you like the activity or event (one meeting or event is NEVER enough): _____

3. Spiritual Organizations and/or Volunteering

One of the most welcoming places to find connections is via spiritual and religious organizations and volunteering (service learning). If you're not religious, think of this as an activity that can nurture your soul. You can find a yoga class or a bible study group or participate in a volunteer organization (think Habitat for Humanity or taking an alternative spring break). Spirituality isn't just about religion. This is time for you to reinforce your beliefs, question your beliefs, and serve others. You might discover that an activity, group, or organization from one of the previous lists can also fall into the spiritual section.

Five spiritual activities or organizations that might interest me:

1. _____   4. _____

2. _____   5. _____

3. _____

These three seem really interesting:

1. _____

2. _____

3. _____

And the winner is (my most favorite at this point):

1. _____

Essential details and info:

Where it meets: _____

When it meets: _____

How you get involved: _____

Potential time commitment: _____

Advisor's name: _____

President's info: _____

Names and contact info of other officers: _____

_____

Who to contact for more info: _____

Your plan for getting involved: _____

_____

How long you will give this before deciding if you like the activity or event (one

meeting or event is NEVER enough): _____

✎ Naked Journal #13: A Naked Adventure

Create your own adventure! Part of being in college is going on adventures. Organize an outing that takes you off campus and into the local community. It can be a trip to the museum, a day at a local park, a train ride to the city. Go on your own adventure off campus and share what you did and what you learned. Did anything you discovered inspire you to now become involved in a specific campus club or organization? Explain.

Naked Exercise #14

Start Your Own Club or Organization

If there isn't something on campus that interests you, instead of complaining, create your own club.

Giving Birth to a Club or Organization

One of the perks of being a student is that you have the power to start clubs and organizations. It can be a new Greek chapter, a barbecue appreciation club, an official campus Justin Bieber fan club, or a tutoring program to help students in the community. Becoming officially recognized can be as easy as filling out paperwork, getting a faculty or staff member to sponsor the organization, and finding a few members.

What's really cool is that official student groups often have access to facilities, activity funds, and leadership opportunities. When I was in college, I was founding member of an improvisational troupe.

Think about what you would consider THE PERFECT club or organization; thinking about it is the first step in *creating* it. Now take the following steps:

What is the procedure to start a club or organization on campus?

_____

_____

_____

What club, activity, or organization is missing on campus that you would like to start?

_____

_____

_____

Is there a similar group or organization on campus? If so, how will yours differ?

_____

_____

_____

What is the group's mission statement?

_____

_____

_____

What types of activities will your group engage in (in other words, what experiences do you want to offer your members)?

_____

_____

_____

How many members would you like to have the first year? _____

The second year? _____

The third year? _____

The fourth year? _____

What is your plan to recruit members?

_____

_____

_____

Who can you ask to advise the group? (list three possible sponsors)

_____

_____

_____

What is your biggest fear about starting a group?

_____

_____

_____

Who can you turn to and what steps can you take to overcome this fear?

_____

_____

_____

✎ **Naked Journal #14:** 1, 2, 3 Push

Write the story of the new group or organization that you have just started (yes, this is fiction). Share the name of your group, the group's mission, how and why you came up with the idea, what inspired you to start the group, how the idea progressed, how you were able to get a faculty sponsor, and how your member recruitment process unfolded. Share three challenges the new group faces and how you can use each of these as opportunities to thrive. Once you come up with your success story, consider turning your dream into a reality.

Rate using a scale of 1–10.

> **1 = Not true → 5 = Somewhat true → 10 = Doesn't get any truer**

_____ I have always wanted to go Greek.

_____ People in fraternities and sororities are self-absorbed and party all the time.

_____ There is an expectation on my campus to go Greek.

_____ I don't want to be friends with someone in a fraternity or sorority.

_____ I would do just about anything to get a bid from a fraternity or sorority.

_____ I can't rush a Greek house because I don't drink, so they'd never want me.

_____ If there aren't any houses that feel right to me, I won't pledge even if I get a bid.

_____ I understand what it means to be a member of a fraternity or sorority.

_____ I won't go through Greek rush because I couldn't deal with not getting picked.

_____ I want to go Greek because they have the best parties.

_____ I won't pledge because I am afraid of hazing.

_____ When I think of Greek life, I think of leadership opportunities.

_____ Greek life is for losers who need to buy friends.

_____ The hottest guys/girls are Greek.

Naked Exercise #15

Greek Life: The Good

You don't have to be Greek to join a fraternity or sorority. You just have to be open to connecting to a community that can lead to lasting friendships, a robust social life, amazing leadership opportunities, and a lifetime of personal and professional connections.

A Quick Request

Some of you will love the idea of fraternity and sorority life and others will absolutely not like the idea of Greek life. Whatever feelings you have about Greek life on campus (assuming your campus has a Greek life), make sure your feelings are based on real information—not rumors or one or two experiences. There are so many aspects to Greek life that aren't often talked about. Usually, those are some of the best parts.

What is your impression of Greek life?

_____

_____

_____

_____

_____

What do you base this impression on? Friends or family who are in Greek organizations? Interactions with members? People outside the Greek system? Something you've seen on TV or read in the newspapers?

_____

_____

_____

List two fraternities and two sororities on campus.

1. _____

2. _____

3. _____

4. _____

Research and find out the average grade point average of the members of the organization.

1. _____

2. _____

3. _____

4. _____

Contact a member and find out what these organizations are doing in terms of

fund-raising activities: _____

volunteer projects: _____

athletics: _____

What leadership positions are held by members of the Greek organizations on campus? (For example, what student leadership positions do Greeks hold in organizations other than their fraternity or sorority?)

_____

_____

_____

What have you learned?

_____

_____

_____

What did you find out that surprised you?

_____

_____

_____

Naked Greek Research

Talk to three members of a fraternity or sorority and ask them their three favorite and least favorite aspects of being a member of the Greek community:

1. Name: _____

Three favorite parts of Greek Life:

    a. _____

    b. _____

    c. _____

Three least favorite parts of Greek Life:

    d. _____

    e. _____

    f. _____

2. Name: _____

Three favorite parts of Greek Life:

  a. _____

  b. _____

  c. _____

Three least favorite parts of Greek Life:

  d. _____

  e. _____

  f. _____

3. Name: _____

Three favorite parts of Greek Life:

  a. _____

  b. _____

  c. _____

Three least favorite parts of Greek Life:

  d. _____

  e. _____

  f. _____

Now, when you hear the words "fraternity" or "sorority," what comes to mind?

_____

_____

_____

✎ Naked Journal #15: Greek Life Exposed

Given what you learned through all of your research on Greek life, what do you think you might be able to get out of it? What newly discovered parts of Greek life might appeal to you? What might you have to gain from joining a fraternity or sorority? Answering doesn't commit you to anything. Use what you learned and come up with an honest answer. If you just can't see yourself participating, share the reasons based on the real information you uncovered.

Naked Exercise #16

Greek Life: The NOT-SO-GOOD

Letters don't define the person—the person defines the letter.

YES—Greek life can provide opportunities to get involved on campus, but it can also create opportunities to get trapped inside the Greek bubble (and maybe even think you're better than the rest of campus). Peer pressure, hazing, and unhealthy behaviors can happen. Easy access to friends and a potent social life can be a dangerous combination.

Answer yes or no to the following statements:

1. My only friends are in my fraternity or sorority. YES / NO

If the answer is YES, how can you use your Greek affiliation to make friends outside of the Greek system?

_____

_____

_____

2. My only organizational involvement is within my chapter. YES / NO

If the answer is YES, how can you use your Greek involvement to help you get involved in other leadership roles on campus?

_____

_____

_____

3. My fraternity brothers or sorority sisters have pressured me to engage in behaviors that I have later regretted. YES / NO

If the answer is YES, what was the behavior? Why did you succumb to the pressure? What could you have done differently? What will you do next time this happens?

_____

_____

_____

4. I will not date certain people because of their Greek affiliation. YES / NO

If the answer is YES, why is it that you won't date certain people?

_____

_____

_____

5. I will not associate with certain people if they are not Greek. YES / NO

If the answer is YES, why is it that you won't associate with people who are not Greek?

_____

_____

_____

6. I dislike people solely based on their Greek affiliation. YES / NO

If the answer is YES, why is it that you feel it's okay to make blanket generalizations? Is there anyone in your chapter who doesn't fit the stereotypes associated with your organization?

_____

_____

_____

7. I rarely attend social functions that aren't Greek affiliated. YES / NO

If the answer is YES, what can you to do attend functions that aren't just Greek affiliated? Why is this important?

_____

_____

_____

8. I feel like I'm better than people because of my Greek affiliation. YES / NO

If the answer is YES, why is it that your affiliation makes you feel like you are better than other people?

_____

_____

_____

9. I have been pressured to do things against my will. YES / NO

If the answer is YES, why do you think you allowed yourself to be pressured?

_____

_____

_____

What could you have said or done to have the power to assert yourself?

_____

_____

_____

When people criticize you or judge you for being Greek, how does that make you feel?

_____

_____

_____

When you judge people outside of the Greek system, how do you think that makes them feel?

_____

_____

_____

If there was ONE thing you'd like to change about your Greek organization, what would it be?

_____

_____

_____

What can you do to contribute to this change?

_____

_____

_____

✎ Naked Journal #16: Your Life Outside the Greek World

A balanced life in college is one where you have friends inside and outside the Greek system. Having balance means living in a world of options. Without options (or friends inside and outside the Greek system), it's easy to feel trapped. What would happen if your organization was suspended or thrown off campus—what would your life be like at college? How would you find your new place? How do you envision your life? Would you have a life? Describe how it would change. What would you do to find new friends? And how would you create a balanced life on campus?

No one ever has the right to humiliate you, force you to do anything that doesn't feel right, or deprive you of sleep. Hazing is against the law and you have every right to alert the authorities.

While Greek life can be a GREAT life, it's not all good. Hazing and social pressures can be two of the biggest obstacles. Some members will do things they regret. Some pledges (future brothers and sisters) will be deprived of sleep, some will be subject to humiliation, some people will be forced to eat or drink something, some will be asked to do something physically grueling, and some will get caught up in the group experience and forget that they have the power to make choices.

If you should ever find yourself doing things you regret, putting others in these situations, or are put in uncomfortable situations where you think you've been hazed, the following exercise can help you organize your thoughts and make some changes.

Alcohol and Social Pressures True or False

1. Members of Greek organizations have a higher rate of alcohol consumption compared to the rest of campus.

   True or False

2. It's possible to be sober and Greek.

   True or False

3. It's possible to avoid peer pressure in a fraternity or sorority.

   True or False

Hazing True or False

1. Hazing is a felony.

   True or False

2. If you witness hazing, you are required to report it, even if people being hazed consent.

   True or False

3. Fifty-five percent of college students involved in clubs, teams, and organizations experience hazing.

   True or False

4. Hazing occurs in, but extends beyond, varsity athletics and Greek letter organizations and includes behaviors that are abusive, dangerous, and potentially illegal.

   True or False

5. Most students who are hazed do not know it's happening.

   True or False

6. Hazing is 100 percent always harmful.

   True or False

7. Alcohol consumption, humiliation, isolation, sleep deprivation, and sex acts are hazing practices that occur in a variety of student groups (Greek and non-Greek).

   True or False

8. If you agree to be hazed with ritualistic alcohol consumption, humiliation, sleep deprivation, and sex acts, it's still considered hazing.

   True or False

9. Students have died as a result of hazing.

   True or False

10. You can report hazing to national chapters and campus officials and remain anonymous.

    True or False

Hazing is defined as:

The term *hazing* means any conduct or method of initiation into any student organization, whether on public or private property, which willfully or recklessly endangers the physical or mental health of any student or other person. Such conduct shall include whipping; beating; branding; forced calisthenics; exposure to weather; forced consumption of any food, liquor, beverage, drug, or other substance; or any other brutal treatment or forced physical activity which is likely to adversely affect the physical health or safety of any such student or other person, or that subjects such student or other person to extreme mental stress, including extended deprivation of sleep or rest or extended isolations.

—Source: Harvard University Extension School

Hazing Worksheet

Should you ever think that you've been hazed, you'll need to be able to recount the details. This worksheet is a resource to help you write down the details and then share them with the appropriate contact on campus or in the national organization.

Describe the hazing incidents you have witnessed or have firsthand knowledge of.

_____

_____

_____

When did this happen (date and time)?

_____

_____

_____

Where did this happen?

_____

_____

_____

Who were the people involved in the incident?

_____

_____

_____

How did this incident make you feel?

_____

_____

_____

Who will you notify on campus to report this incident?

Campus advisor: _____

Email: _____

Phone number: _____

Local police contact: _____

Who will you notify on a national level?

Name of national contact: _____

Email: _____

Phone number: _____

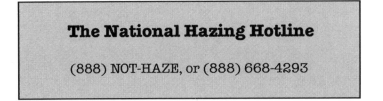

The National Hazing Hotline

(888) NOT-HAZE, or (888) 668-4293

✎ **Naked Journal #17:** Hazing Horror Story

Do some research and search college and local daily newspapers to find a recent victim of college hazing. Write a short paragraph describing what occurred. Then examine why you think it occurred. What do you think group members gain from participating in these rituals? Why do you think that new members allow it to continue? Then examine what could have been done to prevent this from happening and how we can keep it from *ever* happening again. What might change the *culture* of hazing?

Naked Self-Exam Four

Residence Halls: Like a Cruise without the Water

Rate using a scale of 1–10.

> **1** = Not true → **5** = Somewhat true → **10** = Doesn't get any truer

_____ I'm living on campus for convenience, not for the "floor activities."

_____ I don't live on campus, but I have friends who do.

_____ I feel comfortable talking to my resident assistant.

_____ My resident assistant is worthless.

_____ I haven't met anyone I really "click" with in my dorm.

_____ I have met most of the people on my dorm floor.

_____ I'm starting to wish I lived in a different residence hall.

_____ I feel safe in my dorm.

_____ I am very careful to always make sure the door is locked when I leave my room.

_____ I do my part to keep my dorm room and bathroom clean.

_____ My roommate doesn't respect my stuff or my space.

_____ I hate my roommate's hygiene habits.

_____ I securely lock up my valuables (like my iPod, jewelry, and extra money) when I'm not in my room.

_____ I totally trust my roommate and people in my dorm with my things.

_____ I enjoy living on campus.

Naked Exercise #18

Residence Halls: A Quick Education

It's like living at home, but only with one hundred strangers, no parents, and no food in the fridge. Welcome to your residence hall. It's time to get to know your new home and the perks of campus living. Fill out the following information. If you don't know the answers, find someone who does (this can be a great excuse to talk to an attractive neighbor or unfamiliar residence life staff member).

Name of hall: _____

Year resident hall built: _____

Hall is named after: _____

Famous / well-known former residents: _____

_____

_____

_____

The best amenities: _____

_____

_____

_____

Academic resources: _____

_____

_____

_____

Residence Hall Staff

Head of residential life: _____

Residence hall director: _____

Area coordinator: _____

The Rules: Love 'em and Hate 'em

My favorite five rules for the residence halls:

1. _____

2. _____

3. _____

4. _____

5. _____

My least favorite five rules for the residence halls:

1. _____

2. _____

3. _____

4. _____

5. _____

Three rules I WISH were part of living in the residence halls:

1. _____

2. _____

3. _____

✎ Naked Journal #18: Dear Residence Hall...

Write a note to your residence hall expressing what you hope the relationship will be like over the course of the year. What do you want to get out of this relationship? What do you fear the most? What do you hope will not happen?

Example:

Dear Residence Hall,

When I first saw you, I thought you were beautiful. I loved your new floors and counters. I'm sad to learn that you don't have soundproof walls...etc....

Naked Exercise #19

Residence Halls: A Cruise without the Water

At all costs, try to live in a residence hall your freshman year. It's a once, twice, three, or four times in a lifetime experience that will provide you with more good than bad.

Living in the residence halls can be an amazing experience. You get to live in what is often the best location on campus, get to connect with people who share common interests, and don't have to worry about cooking or paying monthly rent or utilities. That said, there can be some not-so-great parts.

But let's start with what you love.

Things I love about living in the residence halls:

I love _the location_   because _I can get up five minutes before class._

I love _____ because _____

I love _____ because _____

I love _____ because _____

I love _____ because _____

I love _____ because _____

Ahhh yes, that felt good. Now let's take a look at the things you don't love (complaining can feel so much more satisfying).

Things I don't love about living in the residence halls:

I do not love _sharing a room with a stranger_ because _he/she is always naked._

I do not love _____ because _____

I do not love _____ because _____

I do not love _____ because _____

I do not love _____ because _____

I do not love _____ because _____

Now, take the WHAT I DON'T LOVE list, and put together a plan on how you'll make it better. For example, if you don't get along with your roommate, talk to your RA (CA, or whatever you call that person), talk to your roommate about the problem, find ways to get out of your room, or change roommates (worst-case scenario).

I don't like living on campus because _I hate having to follow rules like I'm two_

years old.

I can change this by _following the rules like I'm eighteen years old, realizing that some people need them in order for ME to have a better living experience._

* * *

I don't like living on campus because _____

_____

I can change this by _____

_____

I don't like living on campus because _____

_____

I can change this by _____

_____

I don't like living on campus because _____

_____

I can change this by _____

_____

Take one more look at the WHAT I DON'T LOVE list and figure out how you can take away something positive from this experience even if you can't change the experience. For example, living with strangers is great practice for working with strangers—these are great skills for the workplace environment.

Even though I don't love _sharing a bathroom_ _____

I'm learning _to hold it in longer, and where all the awesome bathrooms are on campus._

Even though I don't love _____

I'm learning _____

Even though I don't love _____

I'm learning _____

Even though I don't love _____

I'm learning _____

Even though I don't love _____

I'm learning _____

Even though I don't love _____

I'm learning _____

✎ Naked Journal #19: A Naked Walk

Everyone has preconceived notions when it comes to residential living. For this journal entry, forget assumptions and do a little fact-finding. Take a walking tour of your residence hall and take notes along the way. Look on the bulletin boards, look in the resource center, classrooms, or study lounges, and walk outside. What are three things you never knew about your residence hall that you've discovered? Now, look at the rules and regulations. What are three surprises that you didn't know were part of the rules and regulations?

Naked Exercise #20

The Resident Assistant: Your Personal Assistant

Think of your RA as a big brother/sister and a best friend, only this sibling/friend has the power to write you up and report you (AKA tell on you). And unless your RA smells it, hears it, or steps in it, he or she does not want to write it or report it.

Gotta Get to Know Your Resident Assistant, Community Advisor, or Whatever You Call Him or Her

Your resident assistant is an amazing resource who lives down the hall, on another floor, or close enough to hear it all (and smell it all). Now this is the part of the workbook where you have to put forth some effort and do some of that work I promised. I know your RA is supposed to be the one to get to know you, but *you* are going to be the one to get to know her. Find a time to meet your RA and get the following info:

Resident assistant's name: _____

Hometown: _____

Year in school: _____

Major: _____

Minor: _____

Hobbies / interests:

_____

Favorite music group:

_____

Favorite time of year on campus and why:

_____

Favorite campus tradition and why:

_____

Favorite place to hide ON campus (promise you'll go there too):

_____

Favorite place to hide OFF campus (make same promise):

_____

Favorite place to order in food:

_____

Favorite meal in the dining hall:

_____

Membership in campus clubs and organizations:

_____

_____

Reason he or she became an RA:

_____

_____

Favorite part of being an RA:

_____

_____

Least favorite part of being an RA (answering questions for this project...):

_____

_____

The most challenging part of being an RA:

_____

_____

One thing no one knows about your RA that he or she will reveal to you:

_____

_____

Your resident assistant is there to help you. Most will welcome the opportunity to talk about themselves with you and share their tips and suggestions for getting the most from your college experience. The more you get to know your RA, the more comfortable you'll be seeking him or her out when you need something (see Naked Exercise #4).

Don't just limit yourself to your own RA; get to know others in your residence hall as well. Consider asking some other questions that can help you find your place and get involved on campus (turn to Naked Exercise #3). How can your RA help you? Put together a list of questions you want answers to *right now*. Come on, you know you have some—jot them down here. Then, go ask an RA. Any RA.

1. How hard is it to get written up? _____

2. Can we date RAs? _____

3. _____

4. _____

5. _____

6. _____

✎ Naked Journal #20: RA Role-Playing

If you were an RA, explain how you would do your job. What would be your favorite part of the job? What would be your least favorite part of the job? How would you handle the people who didn't respect you or your authority? How would you make yourself someone your residents could trust? What events would you host for your residents? What would you show them or tell them about that you think they would find useful, important, or fun? (Feel free to share your last answer with your RA. You may find he or she uses your ideas!)

Naked Exercise #21

Meet People in Your Hall without Even Trying

Leave your door open in the residence hall when you're home, and you will meet people. But lock it up when you go to sleep (or leave the room). There's always a chance someone you don't know might end up in your room and in your bed (yep, it happens).

One of the perks of campus living is that it can be easier to make friends. The challenge is that you might not know how to make friends because you've never had to make friends. Childhood friendships just seem to happen. But as you get older, sometimes if you want new friends, you actually have to make an effort to make them (yes, this is the "work" part of this workbook). Sure, there are friendships that will start without much effort, but these might not be the best friendships.

Think about how you can make friends. Hint: People make friends by having shared experiences. Think about experiences you can share as you complete the list, ten ways to meet people with minimal effort.

1. Open your door.

2. Introduce yourself to someone.

3. Invite people to group events (sports, activities, etc.).

4. Attend floor events.

5. Do laundry and ask to borrow detergent.

6. Study in a common area.

7. Eat with someone you don't know.

8. _____

9. _____

10. _____

Now, you might be thinking, "I don't want to look like a jackass." Well, you can use the risk-taking experience in Naked Exercise #9 to help you meet some people and make some friends.

NAKED NOTE: People make friends while putting themselves in rooms with other people. The more rooms you find yourself in, the more people you'll meet.

Friendly Research Project

I love this project. Forget feeling awkward when approaching people, this is an assignment that will force you to meet people.

Here's the assignment: Take a walk in your residence hall and say hi to five people you didn't know before. You can sit down and share a meal with someone. You can talk to someone else while walking to class. You can talk to another you meet in the bathroom (not while he or she is in the stall). Make sure it's five *different* people. If this project intimidates you, plug it into the risk-taking experiment in Naked Exercise #9 and call it one of your risks.

Then get the following info. When you get it, tell them it's an assignment for class. (If they're freshmen, they may have the same assignment—another way you'll make new friends because of this assignment.)

Random Person #1

Name: _____

Hometown: _____

Major: _____

Activities the person is involved with on campus or plans to get involved with:

_____

The reason he or she came to this school:

_____

* * *

Random Person #2

Name: _____

Hometown: _____

Major: _____

Activities the person is involved with on campus or plans to get involved with:

_____

The reason he or she came to this school:

_____

* * *

Random Person #3

Name: _____

Hometown: _____

Major: _____

Activities the person is involved with on campus or plans to get involved with:

_____

The reason he or she came to this school:

_____

✎ Naked Journal #21: Hey, Neighbor!

How did your "friendly research" project go? What were you thinking before the project started? Where did you meet people? What happened that made you uncomfortable? What surprised you? Why was it easier to meet people when it was part of a project as opposed to just meeting people to be friendly? How can you use this experience to help you meet more people in the future? Will you do this again? Explain.

Open your door, open your eyes, open your mouth, and take a walk. You are surrounded by a community waiting to get you involved.

One of the perks of living in a residence hall is that there is always so much going on around you. The problem is that too many people stay in their rooms and don't get involved. From participating in the residence hall association, to attending floor events, to eating in the dining hall, there are so many opportunities to get involved with those who live close to you. But to get involved you need to know what's happening, when it's happening, where it's happening, and how to be a part of what's happening. You also need to be willing to go it alone. And that's where this Naked Exercise begins.

The Floor Event Assignment

For this exercise you are required to attend a floor event or an event happening in the residence halls. I know you're too cool to go to these types of events. That's why this is an assignment. You're not choosing to go. You are required.

Talk to your RA, check out the residence life website, or take a walk around the residence halls and find three events that are coming up in the next month or two (this can be a speaker, a musician, a residence hall association meeting, a T-shirt making class, etc.).

1. _____

2. _____

3. _____

Now, the specifics:

Day of the event: _____

Time of the event: _____

Do you need tickets to attend the event? _____

Who will go with you? _____

(Considering this is an assignment, you can go alone or you can go with someone from class. Remember, going alone doesn't make you a loser. It just makes you someone who doesn't know people because you don't know people. That's part of living in a place where you DO NOT KNOW PEOPLE!! But actually, going alone can make you look extra cool, because you don't need anyone to go with you in order to go or to look cool.)

Post-event worksheet

What event did you attend? _____

_____

What surprised you about this event? _____

_____

What disappointed you? _____

_____

Would you like to do this assignment again? _____

_____

✎ Naked Journal #22: Naked Meal Planning

We all know it's hard to sit down and eat a meal with strangers (and that's not taking into account the campus food). Here's a Naked Exercise designed to help you avoid going hungry and that can help you meet new people on campus while you eat the mystery meat they serve in the cafeteria.

Option 1

Step 1: Eat a meal at a different time and in a different place than usual.

Step 2: Get your meal at the dining hall and find a seat all alone. Remind yourself that you're not a loser, just someone who is hungry. And hungry people need to eat. Give everyone in the dining hall permission to know you're hungry—and NOT a loser. Bring something to focus on. Then eat alone.

Step 3: Describe your experience: What did you feel before, during, and after? Was this hard for you? If so, why? If this was easy, please describe why.

Option 2

Step 1. Eat a meal at a different time and in a different place than usual.

Step 2. Get your meal at the dining hall and find a seat with a person or people you don't know. Remind yourself that you're not a loser, just someone who is hungry. And hungry people need to eat. Give everyone in the dining hall permission to know you're hungry—and NOT a loser. Bring something to focus on, but be prepared to interact with the people at the table. Then eat alone.

Step 3. Describe your experience: What did you feel before, during, and after? Was this hard for you? If so, why? If this was easy, please describe why.

Naked Exercise #23

The Ugly Side of Residential Life

Lock your door, your windows, and put away your electronics when you are not in the room. They might as well have legs because unlocked valuables will walk out your dorm room door.

Let's start off with some difficult true or false questions:

1. Leaving my door unlocked and leaving all my valuables in clear view is an open invitation to steal my stuff.

   True or False

2. Leaving cash on my dresser and leaving the room is as good as putting it in a stranger's pocket.

   True or False

3. Leaving an iPhone, iPad, iPod (or other electronics) in my room with the door open is an iVitation to iSteal my stuff, leaving me feeling iStupid.

   True or False

4. I believe that there are people in the residence halls who will steal my stuff.

   True or False

5. Taking my great grandmother's antique diamond ring to college is the best idea I've had since having unprotected sex with a stranger.

True or False

NOTE: If you need an answer key you might consider moving out.

How much do you value your stuff? How much do you value your safety? If you leave your room unlocked, your room is like a store without price tags. People can shop without paying for stuff. Remember, everything in your dorm room is on display—anyone who comes into your room can check it out or just steal it (then or later). Kleptos are lurking around the corner. You'd be surprised how much you have that can be stolen. So let's take inventory. NOTE: hide this list (or eat it) once you finish it. Otherwise it will give a would-be thief too much info.

Taking Inventory

Top ten items of value:

1. _____ Estimated value: _____

2. _____ Estimated value: _____

3. _____ Estimated value: _____

4. _____ Estimated value: _____

5. _____ Estimated value: _____

6. _____ Estimated value: _____

7. _____ Estimated value: _____

8. _____ Estimated value: _____

9. _____ Estimated value: _____

10. _____ Estimated value: _____

Total replacement costs (assuming everything is stolen):

$ _____

What don't you need at college from your list?

_____ **(Feel free to write "most of it.")**

Precautions to Take

Consider other options for the expensive things you want to have at college.

_____ Do you have a footlocker or way to lock up your valuables?

_____ Do you have a way to mark valuables (an engraver can help)?

_____ Do you have a place on your body that can be used to hide your jewels?

_____ Can you get insurance or do you have insurance for your valuables?

_____ Do you and your roommate have a plan on how to protect your valuables?

_____ If there is a special occasion to wear your jewelry or expensive designer gown, can you go home to pick it up or have a parent send it to you just for the event?

What is your roommate bringing? Don't bring two of the same valuables.

_____

_____

_____

✎ Naked Journal #23: This Workbook Could Get Stolen

For this journal entry you will see how long it takes to get something stolen. Leave your door open and leave five hundred dollars in hundreds on the table. See how long it takes to get stolen. Once it gets taken, put out another five hundred dollars. Then do it one more time. If you still haven't learned, keep doing it until you can see that you can't trust everyone. (NOTE: you are responsible for funding this experiment.)

OR

Talk to three different juniors or seniors who have lived on campus and ask them what's been stolen while they've been in college. Share what they suggest you do to keep your valuables from being taken.

Designated Doodling Space

Instructions: Feel free to draw pictures of your valuables here if you are looking to do some doodling in class. This is not required doodling.

Rate using a scale of 1–10.

> **1** = Not true → **5** = Somewhat true → **10** = Doesn't get any truer

_____ I like my roommate.

_____ I want to get along with my roommate.

_____ My roommate wants to get along with me.

_____ I'm not sure if I like my roommate.

_____ I expect my roommate to like me.

_____ My roommate is a friend or acquaintance from high school.

_____ My roommate and I have already made a plan for how we will do things in the room and solve problems, etc.

_____ I know that my roommate and I will never get along.

_____ I'm uncomfortable with the differences between myself and my roomie.

_____ I am cleaner than my roommate *and* do more to keep the room clean than my roommate.

_____ It's just as much my room as my roommate's, so I should be able to keep it any way that I want.

_____ My roommate is too "conservative" and I feel restricted by the rules he or she wants me to follow.

_____ It would not bother me if my roommate's boyfriend or girlfriend hangs out in our room a lot—the more the merrier.

_____ I want my privacy and I don't want other people spending a lot of time in our room.

_____ I just ignore my roommate when he or she is drunk or high. I don't want to get involved in his or her problems.

_____ It doesn't bother me that my roommate parties heavily—that's what college is about for some people.

_____ It's not my responsibility to get involved in my roommate's problems.

_____ If I thought there was something wrong with my roommate, I would get help immediately.

_____ I think my roommate has a serious problem with alcohol, drugs, or depression.

_____ I'm extremely considerate of my roommate.

_____ I could win BEST roommate of the year.

Naked Exercise #24

The Ultimate Roommate Rule

Roommates who want to get along will find a way to get along. Roommates who don't want to get along will not get along. It's really just that simple.

The Big Naked Problem

Here's the deal—everyone wants a roommate situation to be the PERFECT one. But the big problem isn't that there are problems, it's that roommates do not tell each other when there's a problem. They will talk to friends, family, strangers, post notes on Facebook, blog, and text but RARELY honestly address things with the person it concerns. Too often secret issues build up over time and resentment builds. This is when little problems blow up into huge problems. Why does this happen?

Roommates don't like conflict. But I can tell you with 100 percent certainty that no two (three, or four) people living together will ALWAYS get along. It's true of spouses, significant others, friends, and strangers.

Spirited and honest conversation is part of a healthy relationship. But roommates must first set up the dynamics so that uncomfortable conversations are not all-out confrontations. This starts by all roommates giving one another permission to share the truth and hear the truth in a timely manner.

Whether you are living in a double, triple, or quadruple suite, there are three things you must do in order to live in harmony. Use the contract on the next page and you will be guaranteed (well, almost) a happy, healthy, and comfortably uncomfortable living situation. That is, if EVERYONE agrees to follow the three Naked Clauses in the roommate contract.

—The Roommate Contract—

Naked Clause I: Getting Along Clause

Naked Clause II: Reasonable Expectations Clause

Naked Clause III: The Uncomfortable Clause

Naked Clause I: Getting Along Clause

Roommates who want to get along will find a way to get along. Too many times, roommates judge or dislike each other before ever meeting. In order to make it clear that you want to get along, all roommates must agree to the following:

Roommate #1

I, _____, Do / Do not (circle one) want to get along.

Roommate #2

I, _____, Do / Do not (circle one) want to get along.

Roommate #3

I, _____, Do / Do not (circle one) want to get along.

Roommate #4

I, _____, Do / Do not (circle one) want to get along.

Naked Clause II: Reasonable Expectations Clause

One of the biggest obstacles roommates face is that one, both, or all roommates move into a room with the expectation that being a roommate = being a best friend. Being a roommate does not equal being a best friend. A roommate is responsible for paying a portion of the rent and making living on campus more affordable. That's it. A roommate is required to be nothing more than someone who shares space and respects the others and their things. Anything else is a bonus. All roommates must agree to the following:

Roommate #1

I, _____, give you permission to NOT be my best friend (although if that happens, I'll consider it an added bonus). My only expectation is for you to be someone who shares space with me and respects me and my stuff.

Roommate #2

I, _____, give you permission to NOT be my best friend (although if that happens, I'll consider it an added bonus). My only expectation is for you to be someone who shares space with me and respects me and my stuff.

Roommate #3

I, _____, give you permission to NOT be my best friend (although if that happens, I'll consider it an added bonus). My only expectation is for you to be someone who shares space with me and respects me and my stuff.

Roommate #4

I, _____, give you permission to NOT be my best friend (although if that happens, I'll consider it an added bonus). My only expectation is for you to be someone who shares space with me and respects me and my stuff.

Naked Clause III: The Uncomfortable Clause

Too many times, roommates keep their honest feelings a secret because they want to avoid conflict. They can't see that living together with a stranger (or friend) can naturally be uncomfortable. Again, no boyfriend/girlfriend or husband/wife or best friends who live together are ALWAYS happy. Therefore, all roommates must agree to the following:

If you do something that makes me uncomfortable, I must tell you within twenty-four to forty-eight hours or I will NOT be allowed to tell you. If I do something that makes you uncomfortable, you must tell me within twenty-four to forty-eight hours. If neither roommate expresses himself or herself within twenty-four to forty-eight hours, we are NOT allowed to talk to ANYONE about the problem. We all promise NOT to fight, but we will listen, respect each others' opinions, and try to get along (see Clause I and Clause II).

Uncomfortable issues can be, but are not limited to

- making too much noise
- having guests over
- sharing food
- expelling gas in the room
- having sex in the room (with someone or alone) with roommates present
- being messy (leaving stuff around)
- being dirty (leaving old food and dirty underwear around)
- having friends over
- getting up too early
- staying up too late
- partying in the room
- wearing your roommate's clothes
- borrowing your roommate's underwear
- using your roommate's stuff without asking first
- not respecting your roommate's stuff
- lounging in the nude
- your roommate's sexual orientation
- your roommate's race, religion, or ethnic background

Agreed: YES / NO (circle)

Roommate #1: Agreed _____

Roommate #2: Agreed _____

Roommate #3: Agreed _____

Roommate #4: Agreed _____

Bonus Clause: In Case of Emergency

Everyone needs to look after one another. Sometimes, being away from friends and family can lead to unforeseen situations. That's where the Bonus Clause comes in. The In Case of an Emergency Bonus Clause states:

I give permission to my roommate(s) to contact my parents via cell phone in case of an emergency. This is something you can do only if you think I'm in imminent danger or in case of an emergency.

Roommate #1

Agree to emergency clause: YES / NO

Emergency contact's name: _____

Emergency contact's cell phone: _____

Emergency email: _____

Roommate #2

Agree to emergency clause: YES / NO

Emergency contact's name: _____

Emergency contact's cell phone: _____

Emergency email: _____

Roommate #3

Agree to emergency clause: YES / NO

Emergency contact's name: _____

Emergency contact's cell phone: _____

Emergency email: _____

Roommate #4

Agree to emergency clause: YES / NO

Emergency contact's name: _____

Emergency contact's cell phone: _____

Emergency email: _____

✎ Naked Journal #24: The Entry from Hell

We've all heard the expression "Roommate from hell." While we are all so focused on everyone else doing things wrong, rarely do we think that *we* could be the roommate from hell. Describe yourself and what personal characteristics or habits could possibly make you the roommate from hell. What can you do about these tendencies to avoid being the worst roommate in the world?

Naked Exercise #25

Enforcing the Roommate Contract

Focus on what you and your roommate have in common and you will have a much better chance of getting along. Focus on your differences and you will soon find yourself with a different roommate.

How to Get Along

The way roommates get along is for all roommates to make an effort to get along. This all starts with attitude. Bad roommates have bad attitudes. Good roommates have good attitudes (see the pattern). Instead of focusing on all the things you dislike about your roommate and all the things that will make this relationship *not* work, take a step back and focus on things you have in common. Chances are, you and your roommate are both very much alike and, in many ways, very different. First, identify those characteristics that your roommate shares with you. (For example, my roommate is a neat freak and I'm a neat freak.)

Qualities We Share

I Am...   My Roommate Is...

_____   _____

_____   _____

_____   _____

_____   _____

Use this list to find common ground. The fact that you share at least some things in common gives you a place to start should any problems arise. If you can relate on some level, then you have the potential to use that connection to address the differences. Which is what you will now do. (Don't pretend you didn't know it was coming...)

Now, the Differences

Identify those character traits in which you and your roommate diverge—ways in which you just don't see eye to eye. (Maybe eye to shoulder isn't so bad. Eye to belly button is getting scary. Eye to knee is bad news. Eye to toe—let's not even go there.)

Qualities We Do Not Share

I Am...   My Roommate Is...

_____   _____

_____   _____

_____   _____

_____   _____

The second list is the one that will present a challenge. If all roommates have signed the contract in the previous Naked Exercise, you should be able to address the issues that make life uncomfortable. That said, you have to be willing to compromise (and so does your roommate(s)). Again, just because something makes you uncomfortable doesn't mean that someone has to stop what they're doing. If you bring up issues and your roommate is willing to listen or work to get along (or you are unwilling to work to get along), it might be helpful to bring in your residential life staff. Residential life staff are likely to carry more weight. They can also help discuss those issues that fall into the "too uncomfortable to discuss category" (i.e., the masturbating roommate). Be sure to do this with your RA so you can have a mediator and a witness and expectations and stipulations for behavior. Then new rules can be noted in your contract.

✎ Naked Journal #25: The Naked Contract

A contract is only as strong as the signers' commitment to follow it. Take time to explain what a contract means to you. Are you committed to following this? How will you and your roommates enforce the rules? What will happen if one (or more roommates) doesn't follow through? What's the protocol? Share this with all your roommates and come to an agreement about the agreement. When you're finished sharing, explain how this went. What did you learn about yourself? What did you learn about your roommate(s)?

Naked Exercise #26

Roommate Conflict Worksheet

It's worth mentioning one more time: even the very BEST roommates will *not* always get along. Not the happiest spouses, not the best boyfriends and girlfriends, and not strangers living together will get along 100 percent of the time. When something comes up that makes you uncomfortable (and it will), it helps to talk through it with yourself before confronting your roommate with it. This worksheet and exercise is designed to help you think it through before talking it out.

So What's the Problem?

Issue	Proposed Solution

Before assuming your roommate is the problem, ask yourself, "Have I been the perfect roommate?" Are you holding up your end of the deal, or are you perhaps letting some things slide? Are you always considerate regarding noise, cleaning common areas, having guests over, and locking up when you leave? Do you retaliate and hold a grudge because you've been keeping things that make you uncomfortable from your roommate?

It's important to do a self-check before requiring the same of someone else. Perhaps you can think of ways to do better on your part, and when you share your intentions with your roommate, your requests will be viewed much more positively.

I can be a better roommate by:

_____

_____

_____

Did my roommate make me uncomfortable on purpose? YES / NO

If answering YES, please explain how you know this was intentional (being a mind-reader is not a valid reason).

_____

_____

_____

Could there be a misunderstanding? Could this be something your roommate thought was reasonable and normal? Could it be that your roommate was being himself or herself and didn't think you would be bothered?

_____

_____

_____

Is this something you need to discuss? Could there be something you can do differently or is there a different way to look at this situation without having to discuss the problem?

_____

_____

_____

If you decide you must discuss the issue with your roommate, complete the following:

1. Best time to discuss (hint: always while someone is sober and fully clothed):

_____

_____

_____

2. Best place to discuss (hint: never in front of other people):

_____

_____

_____

3. How I would want my roommate to approach me with this situation:

_____

_____

_____

4. How I will communicate the problem:

_____

_____

_____

5. What I will do if he or she attacks me verbally or goes on the defensive:

_____

_____

_____

NOTE: Avoid telling someone what *he or she* did to upset you. Instead, speak about how *you* feel and how important it is for you to have an honest relationship with your roommate. Acknowledge that this makes you uncomfortable to share, but you really want to get along and hope your roommate wants to get along. Here is a sample script to demonstrate:

> YOU: *I know we agreed that if something makes either of us uncomfortable we're supposed to talk about it. There's something I need to bring up. Is this a good time to talk about it?*
> · Share what happened.
> · Share how it made you feel.
> · Share that you only wanted to say something because you want to get along.

NOTE: Some roommates will get defensive, mad, or embarrassed. Give your roommate time and permission to respond without intensifying the situation. Don't get into a shouting match. Just listen and say, "I'm sorry you feel that way" if your roommate attacks; do not antagonize. Ask when you can talk about it without arguing.

When to Seek Professional Mediation

If the situation is too uncomfortable, have a residence life professional sit in or approach your roommate on your behalf. You should also use your residence life professional to help you to go through the conflict resolution worksheet.

If Your Roommate Freaks Out

Wait until he or she cools down. Then state that you want to get along and ask your roommate if he or she wants to get along. Most will. But if your roommate swears at you or throws something at you, that's a strong indication that your roommate definitely does not want to get along.

✎ Naked Journal #26: Role-Playing

Review the following ten situations that could arise in a roommate situation. Pick three of these and write down how to approach each situation without turning a conversation into a confrontation. If you have a different situation you would like to address, use #11.

What do you do when your roommate...

1. has a significant other spend the night and tells you to leave?

2. has sex in the room (with someone or alone) while you're sleeping?

3. keeps you up at night or wakes you up too early?

4. talks on the phone ALL the time when you're in the room?

5. brings friends over to party without asking you?

6. borrows your clothing without asking?

7. is rude to your friends when they visit the room?

8. has horrible body odor and desperately needs to shower?

9. is NEVER in the room?

10. ignores you?

11. _____

Naked Exercise #27

The Judgmental Roommate

Avoid judging your roommate based on first impressions. Sure, first impressions last a lifetime, but sometimes they're the wrong impression.

Judging Has Never Been So Easy & Efficient

Twenty years ago, roommates had to wait to meet or talk on the phone to judge and generalize about each other. Today, there's Facebook and Google to help speed up the process.

First impressions can last forever, but that doesn't mean they're accurate. Let's start with YOU.

The truth is that YOU may be someone's random roommate. Someone might have the *completely* wrong impression of you based on the information you (or someone else) have presented to them via Facebook.

What impression might a new roommate form about you? How might someone judge you and get it wrong? Take a look at your social networking profile and see just how easy it could be to come to the wrong conclusions.

Your Profile

Interested in: _____

How this can be misinterpreted: _____

Looking for: _____

How this can be misinterpreted: _____

Political views: _____

How this can be misinterpreted: _____

Activities: _____

How this can be misinterpreted: _____

Favorite books: _____

How this can be misinterpreted: _____

Favorite music: _____

How this can be misinterpreted: _____

Favorite TV shows: _____

How this can be misinterpreted: _____

Favorite movies: _____

How this can be misinterpreted: _____

Favorite quotes: _____

How this can be misinterpreted: _____

About me: _____

How this can be misinterpreted: _____

Groups/Causes/Pages you like: _____

How this can be misinterpreted: _____

What your pictures show: _____

How this can be misinterpreted: _____

Things people have written on your wall: _____

How this can be misinterpreted: _____

So, before you judge others based on similar information, consider your own and how accurate (or inaccurate) it might be.

Naked First Impressions

A first impression can be a funny memory when later you reflect with your best friend how much you hated him or her when you first met. (Wait until you're friends for a good year before sharing how much you hated him or her.) Now think about your new roommate and the thoughts that may be coloring your interactions and experiences with him or her.

- What have you based your impressions on?
- Are these fair things upon which to judge someone?
- Did you jump to conclusions too quickly?

My roommate is _____

I assume this because _____

Confirmed and 100 percent true? YES / NO

* * *

My roommate is _____

I assume this because _____

Confirmed and 100 percent true? YES / NO

* * *

My roommate is _____

I assume this because _____

Confirmed and 100 percent true? YES / NO

* * *

My roommate is _____

I assume this because _____

Confirmed and 100 percent true? YES / NO

* * *

My roommate is _____

I assume this because _____

Confirmed and 100 percent true? YES / NO

Given that you've already granted your roommate permission to NOT be your new best friend, you just need to find enough reason to coexist. If you are struggling to get along with your roommate, work to find the good points (there must be SOMETHING good!). Maybe you can find enough motivation to identify some good qualities about your roommate.

Roommate's best qualities:

1. _____

2. _____

3. _____

4. _____

5. _____

✎ Naked Journal #27: The Worst First Impression

When have you totally misjudged someone in the past? Share the story of how you met someone for the first time and didn't connect, but later found that you had a close connection. What is similar or different about this meeting compared to your roommate experience? Do any of the same lessons apply?

Designated Doodling Space

Suggested doodle: draw a picture of your perfect room design and/or layout.

Naked Exercise #28

The Best Friend Roommate

There's so much more to lose than there is to be gained by living with your best friend from high school. But if you live with a good friend from high school (not what I advise in *The Naked Roommate* book, see chapter 3, Tip 17), let's make this the best situation.

Clearly you like your best friend. You think he or she is great, fun to be with, and someone who's got your back (that's why he or she is your good or best friend).

BUT...there are things that bother you about your friend. It doesn't have to be anything major, but let's admit it, your friend has irritating quirks, odd habits, annoying behaviors, and strange odors that you tolerate because you're best friends.

First take a look at the similarities and differences between you and your friend.

Similarities between us: _____

Differences between us: _____

Similarities between us: _____

Differences between us: _____

Similarities between us: _____

Differences between us: _____

Similarities between us: _____

Differences between us: _____

While both can enhance a friendship, both can also detract from it when experienced continuously 24/7 in a very tight space with new life stressors to deal with. Consider how each item you listed for *both* categories might be a challenge to your ability to

- focus and study for classes
- pursue your own interests and activities

- meet new people to add to your circle of friends
- try different things
- enjoy times of peace and quiet
- let loose and have fun
- keep your part of the room as you like it
- live a relaxed and stress-free life

Naked Quirks/Behaviors

While it may seem comforting and safe to live with people you are already friends with when you begin your new college adventure, too much of a good thing can ruin what you've built together over the time your friendship has developed. Do this exercise for any of your current friends whom you are considering sharing a teeny tiny, cramped room with. (NOTE: Hide this from your friend!!!)

Quirk/Habit/Behavior: _____

Makes me feel: _____

Quirk/Habit/Behavior: _____

Makes me feel: _____

Quirk/Habit/Behavior: _____

Makes me feel: _____

Quirk/Habit/Behavior: _____

Makes me feel: _____

Now imagine how the quirk/habit/behavior might be magnified by having to deal with them 24/7. Picture the layout of your chosen residence hall: the dimensions of the room, how the beds and desks are situated, what the sink and bathroom set-up is. What might life be like when you are in such close quarters and have to function at the most personal level around this person ALL THE TIME? Consider all the items on the previous list as well.

College Goal	Challenges Related to Living with a Friend
Focus and study for classes	_____
Pursue your own interests	_____
Meet new people and create friendships	_____
Spend time with other friends	_____
Try different things and seek changes	_____
Enjoy times of peace and quiet	_____
Let loose and have fun	_____
Keep your part of the room as you like it	_____
Have your personal space and time	_____
Date and develop romantic relationships	_____
Live a relaxed and stress-free life	_____

The Best Fix for the Best Friend

So, you're already committed to living together with your best friend. How do you make sure you can be roommates and friends? How can you get through the challenges in this exercise? The answer is in the roommate contract. YES, best friends NEED to fill out that roommate contract. When you fill it out, you can bring up the issues that concern you. If you can't talk about them before you are roommates, how can you expect to talk about them once you start living together?

List of issues I need to discuss before living with my close friend:

1. _____

2. _____

3. _____

4. _____

5. _____

✎ Naked Journal #28: Should It Go Bad

Imagine you lived with a good friend and it didn't turn out as planned. Share how you feel about losing this relationship. Share what you will miss about this friendship. Share what you've been able to learn by going through this experience. Share what you've missed by not living with someone else. Write about the worst case scenario and why it didn't work out as planned.

NOTE: Once you finish this, do the opposite should you live with a good friend.

Naked Exercise #29

The Lesbian, Gay, Bisexual, or Transgender Roommate (Pick One)

If you're not gay, living with someone who is gay is a once-in-a-lifetime experience. If you are gay, living with someone who's straight is a once-in-a-lifetime experience. Either way can be a lifetime experience.

The Gay/Hetero/Bi/Transgender Truth

If you buy into the assumption that roughly 10 percent of students on campus are lesbian, gay, bisexual, or transgender, there's a reasonable chance some heterosexual roommates will have gay roommates and some gay roommates will have hetero roommates. And yes, some gay and hetero roommates will live together too. Now that this is out in the open, let's dig deeper into the gay/lesbian/hetero roommate exercise.

If You Are the Straight Roommate...

Are you prepared to live with someone who is gay? Why or why not? These are questions you need to answer.

At the least, it will help you cope with something perhaps unfamiliar or uncomfortable, and at best, it could enable you to develop a wonderful (platonic) relationship with your roommate and maybe even find a lifelong friend.

In order for this to happen, should you share a room or suite with someone who has a different sexual orientation, you need to be up front and honest with *yourself* about how you really feel about things. Here's your chance.

First, identify any people you have known who are gay, lesbian, or bisexual, or people you think might be (and identify why you think that). Identify what characteristics they exhibit that you believe express their homosexuality. In other words, what do they do that they only do because they are gay?

Person #1 LGBT behaviors: _____

_____

Person #2 LGBT behaviors: _____

_____

Person #3 LGBT behaviors: _____

_____

Time for another honest self-reflection. Are the LGBT behaviors you listed *really* related to the person's sexual orientation, or are you just seeing it that way? Have you ever observed someone who wasn't gay doing or saying the same thing or acting in the same way? Now go back and cross out any answers you wrote down that really don't count as specific LGBT behaviors.

If what remains on your list does not cover all of the behaviors that you associate with people who have a different sexual orientation than you, keep it on the list. Write everything down that you believe you might see if you spent time hanging around people who were LGBT. Again, be honest—no one will read this (assuming you don't lose this, blog it, or share it on Facebook—don't do that).

LGBT Behaviors (My Complete List)

_____

_____

_____

Assuming your list is accurate (which you need to reflect on: are these things objectively true, or are you just seeing them this way?), what is your reaction to these behaviors? Do you embrace them fully as reflecting an alternate lifestyle and the many differences between people? Or do you struggle to get past all of the aspects of these differences that you simply cannot understand? Answer the following questions as completely as you can.

What do you want to know about these differences?

_____

_____

_____

What makes you uncomfortable being around someone who exhibits these behaviors?

_____

_____

_____

What is it that you *fear* in people who are different in this way? Why?

_____

_____

_____

How do you think your life would be affected by having an LGBT roommate?

_____

_____

_____

You've already heard this many times, but this is a good place to say it again: College is the place to have new experiences and get to know different people. Life in college should help you step out of your comfort zone and help you to look at the world differently. It should challenge the beliefs and perceptions you have held to this point in your life. It prepares you to go out into a diverse world where you *will* meet all kinds of people with all kinds of beliefs and all kinds of lifestyles, whom you *will* interact with and work with and perhaps even develop close relationships with. There's no time to lose—begin your transformation now!

If these questions have made you uncomfortable and worried, read up on the areas in which you are confused, unfamiliar, or just plain scared of facing. Learn the facts. Try to adjust your thinking. Embrace the opportunity to expand your circle of friends.

If You Are the Lesbian, Gay, Bisexual, or Transgender Roommate...

Are you prepared to live with a heterosexual roommate? Are you prepared to live with a gay roommate? While you may have lots of apprehensions about your upcoming move, start to think about it as an opportunity to be authentic.

Consider how you will present yourself to others without hiding who you really are. Think about people on campus who can help and support you. Remember that it's not a requirement that you inform people of your sexual orientation upon the first meeting—just don't feel like it is something you must actively suppress, if that's not for you.

Use the following prompts to help you prepare for your transition to college. What kind of LGBT resources are available on campus?

_____

_____

_____

Things I will bring to decorate my room that reflect who I am are:

_____

_____

_____

When asked if I am dating anyone, I will say:

_____

_____

_____

If asked if I have a boyfriend or girlfriend, I will say:

_____

_____

_____

If given the opportunity to share about being LGBT, I would tell people:

_____

_____

_____

If someone reacts negatively (fearfully, abusively) to learning that I am LGBT, I will:

_____

_____

_____

Who are people I can turn to for help and guidance before I arrive and while on campus? (Hint: See if there are LGBT student organizations, a center on campus, and advisors.)

1. _____   4. _____

2. _____   5. _____

3. _____   6. _____

Make sure your RA is on this list. Res life staff are trained in how to help students adapt to the new demands and challenges of living with new and different people—no matter what their background. You can find a wonderful ally in your (or any) resident assistant in your dorm.

You *will* find friends. You *will* find compassion. You *can* be who you are. Embrace it, and through it make the most of your college experience.

✎ Naked Journal #29: Temporary Sex Change

If you're lesbian, gay, or bisexual, imagine that you are straight. If you're heterosexual, imagine that you are gay, lesbian, or bisexual.

Now that you've altered your sexual orientation, take a moment and express how you think you would feel about living with someone new. What would be your fears? What do you think your roommate's fears might be? What would make you curious? How would you handle the situation (and no, moving out and avoiding it is NOT an option). What would you do if your roommate was less than accepting? How would you react if your roommate was completely accepting?

Naked Exercise #30

The Noisy, Naughty, Nasty, Drunk, High, Horrible, and Inconsiderate Roommate from Hell

If your roommate has sex while you're in the room, feel free to say something, take a closer look, or invite friends over. It's your room too!

Sometimes a roommate situation will be less than perfect. For example, a roommate might do something that falls under the category of noisy, nasty, or naughty. It could be a boyfriend or girlfriend who never leaves. It could be a drinking problem that leads to a passed-out, peeing roommate. Or it could just be someone who is dirty and nasty. Should it happen, it might shock or offend you. But as long as you have an agreement in place, you will always be able to talk about uncomfortable situations.

Yes, you have the right to live in peace and function around your "home" without undue stress and discomfort caused by the other person. But your roommate also has that same right. This will mean finding ways to compromise and reach a middle ground. It also means picking your battles and addressing the big problems—the ones you really can't live with.

If you are facing some of those, list them here:

Big Problem	My Attempt to Solve It
_____	_____
_____	_____
_____	_____
_____	_____
_____	_____

Take this list to your residence life staff so that you can show him or her what you've already done (hopefully reflecting the recommended approach of open, honest communication that includes respectful dialogue and a sincere recognition of personal differences, but with the strong statement that THIS IS NOT ACCEPTABLE TO ME!). Once they see you've made an honest effort, you can ramp up the intensity of your strategies. You can also use the roommate conflict sheet to work through the situation.

One thing worth mentioning: oftentimes, a roommate who is noisy, nasty, and naughty may appear to NOT want to get along but is actually a roommate who is secretly dealing with bigger issues (sometimes, mental health issues). If you ever have a roommate who doesn't want to get along or appears to be out of control, perhaps something serious is making that roommate be particularly aggressive or detached. This can be a good place for you to record behavior.

Examples of behavior that can indicate a bigger problem:

- Drinking to the point of passing out
- Having sex with multiple, random partners
- Sleeping all the time
- Not sleeping at all
- Not bathing or caring for personal hygiene
- Not cleaning
- Not caring about classes
- Threatening you
- Doing drugs
- Hurting oneself
- Never leaving the room
- Not talking

Use this space to record what you've noticed and share this with a residence life professional or health professional on campus.

Roommate's behavior that makes me uncomfortable:

_____

_____

_____

When I first started noticing it:

_____

_____

_____

Specifically what I've observed:

_____

_____

_____

People you can alert on campus to help your roommate:

1. _____   3. _____

2. _____   4. _____

✎ Naked Journal #30: What You Never Expected to See, Hear, or Smell

This is one of my favorite journal entries. This is when you get to share the craziest, strangest, wildest, and wackiest thing you've ever witnessed as a roommate. Please don't use any names. Just share the story of what you NEVER expected to see, hear, or smell. Please send a copy to Harlan@HelpMeHarlan.com (subject: Crazy Roommate Stories from Journal). Maybe I can include it in a blog or future project. Thanks!

THE NAKED STUDY SECTION

Howdy! Cynthia here...

I know you've been hanging out with Harlan for a while, but I thought I'd step in and get you thinking about the academic part of your college experience, based on my experience as a college professor (plus the advice and tips of many students just like you). This section will prompt exploration of your habits and approaches to being a student, and provide insight as to how you can enhance some of your scholastic techniques. If you are just starting your first semester, your college GPA is a perfect 4.0! If it's as important for you to do well academically as it is for you to make new friends and discover the person you've always wanted to be, stick with me for this section and you'll have a strong foundation for what it takes to stay in college so you can do those things and more!

So that you can get geared up for the good stuff to come, here's what we're going to cover during this naked study section:

- Time management
- Classroom savvy
- Taking top-notch notes
- Reading remedies
- Studying strategies

Naked Self-Exam Six

Time to Talk about Time

Rate using a scale of 1–10.

1 = Not true → **5** = Somewhat true → **10** = Doesn't get any truer

_____ I'm excellent at managing my time.

_____ I can never get everything done that I need to do for my classes.

_____ I am not getting enough sleep.

_____ I feel like I have much more time than I had in high school.

_____ I procrastinate frequently.

_____ Whenever I have time between classes, I review notes or read an assignment for class.

_____ I don't have time to get involved on campus.

_____ Between school demands and my job, I have no time left for a social life.

_____ I thrive on being constantly busy and fill all my time with school and other activities.

_____ I work best under pressure.

_____ I feel overwhelmed with all my responsibilities.

_____ I have no idea how to schedule my time effectively.

_____ I make sure I have time to socialize, even if I don't keep up with my schoolwork.

_____ I make sure to complete reading and other assignments the day they are assigned.

_____ To keep up with all my responsibilities, I use some form of a planner (written, electronic, etc.).

_____ I could benefit from learning strategies to help me manage my time.

_____ I tend to over-commit myself.

_____ Sometimes I miss due dates because I've lost track of time.

Naked Time Management

Taming Your Time

The number-one key to college success is time management. When you take control of what you do, when you do it, and for how long, you are much more likely to get the grades you want while you take part in campus social life, and enjoy your hobbies in your free time.

How you scored the items in the previous survey should give you a sense of how far you have to go in order to tame your time. To keep this intro short (for the sake of time), let's jump right into this one.

The Stress Test

What stresses you out? Don't hold back here. Feel free to unload. Make a list of all the things related to your time that cause you anxiety.

Things that I have to do right now for my classes, that I don't feel I have time to do:

1. _____

2. _____

3. _____

4. _____

5. _____

Things that I have to do right now for my family, that I don't feel I have time to do:

1. _____

2. _____

3. _____

4. _____

5. _____

Things that I have to do right now for my friends, that I don't feel I have time to do:

1. _____

2. _____

3. _____

4. _____

5. _____

Things that I have to do right now for my extracurricular activities, that I don't feel I have time to do:

1. _____

2. _____

3. _____

4. _____

5. _____

Things that I have to do right now for my job, that I don't feel I have time to do:

1. _____

2. _____

3. _____

4. _____

5. _____

Things that I have to do for myself, that I don't feel I have time to do:

1. _____

2. _____

3. _____

4. _____

5. _____

Time to Take Control!

Now that you've taken all this time to write this all down, do you feel more stressed or less?

The main source of stress that you feel in college comes from a sense that *you are not in control*. That's right—it's all about having control—control over your time, which is control over your life. When you believe you have more to do than there is time to do it, you panic, thinking that your life is moving forward and leaving you (and all your unfinished tasks) behind. The reason time management is key to your success is because it puts you in control. And with that, you can relax and productively tackle your responsibilities.

Naked Exercise #31

Time Wasters

What's the greatest threat to good time management? Answer: WASTING TIME! It's like eating that extra piece of double chocolate-chip cheesecake with whipped cream—it's sure fun while you are doing it, but you will really regret it later when you're trying to fit into your skinny jeans or auditioning shirtless for the next season of *Jersey Shore*.

Take a few minutes and do yourself a favor. Identify all the ways you routinely waste time. I've listed a few to get you started.

_____ Watch television because it's on, not because I'm interested in the show.

_____ Sit with my textbook for long periods when my thoughts are somewhere else.

_____ Go out with my friends for lunch or dinner even though I just ate.

_____ Work my farm on Facebook and play Angry Birds on my phone.

_____ Chat with friends on Facebook.

_____ Anything I do on Facebook. (They have yet to complete the Facebook study assistance module.)

Now you're on your own:

1. _____

2. _____

3. _____

C'mon, I know you have more than this. Even *I* have more than this, and I'm a pretty good time manager!

4. _____

5. _____

6. _____

7. _____

8. _____

9. _____

10. _____

Now that you've made your list, I want to make sure you are clear about what *wasting time* really means. It doesn't mean just anything that you mind doing that isn't studying (which sometimes people think I mean, given that I'm a professor). It means **doing something you aren't really interested in doing, or you aren't particularly enjoying doing.**

Time wasters are things that take away valuable time from the things you need or want to do, that give you nothing in return.

Think about that last statement again. *They give you nothing in return.* So you might ask how it is anyone would purposefully choose to waste time. Well, typically we don't set out to waste time, it just happens. Some of us have a gift for it (or access to Facebook). Here are some reasons you might find yourself wasting time:

- Your roommate or friend draws you into what he or she is doing simply because you are around.
- You don't have a plan for what to do with your time and you end up doing something unexpected—but unproductive and unenjoyable.
- You persist in doing something beyond the point where you are getting something out of it.
- You have difficulty making a decision as to what to do.
- You aren't motivated to take the first step to do something productive or fun.
- You let others determine what you do with your time (family, friends, boyfriend/girlfriend, roommate).
- You don't think about how you are using your time until it's too late and you wish you had more of it.
- You make a plan, but then you don't stick to it (don't you hate when that happens?).
- You might be dealing with a medical issue (this includes mental-health issues).

Can you think of other reasons you end up wasting time? Again, I need some serious honesty here. Until you realize that you are doing it, and why you are doing it (wasting time, that is), you won't be able to stop it.

Things that cause me (that's you, not me) to waste time (feel free to borrow some of my examples if they apply to you):

1. _____

2. _____

3. _____

4. _____

5. _____

Prioritizing Is a Top Priority

So how do you start this time management thing? First, you need to prioritize. Go back through each list you made earlier of what you need to do right now, and indicate the importance of completing each item (what needs to be done first, second, third, etc.).

How can you be sure you've got things in the right order? Consider the two following factors: **due dates** and **relative consequences**. Due dates refer to timeliness—if something must be turned in, studied for, or paid for, then they should take priority. Weigh this factor with what would happen if those things don't get done immediately (or by their due date). Are the consequences big? Will you lose points? Get a grade of zero? Get charged a fee? Miss out on an opportunity? Hurt someone's feelings? Go to jail? (What could you possibly have done where you might go to jail!)

P.S. Don't Forget the Fun!

I realize a lot of this section will focus on your personal responsibilities *to other people*: your professors (for class), your organizations (for meetings, leadership roles, practices), your friends (their social needs), your family (their expectations), etc. But you can't overlook the importance of your own need for fun and enjoyment. Don't be confused. Wasting time and having fun are NOT the same thing!

Naked Exercise #33

How You Have Fun (While Fully Clothed)

To get you in the right frame of mind, I want you to write down your favorite ways to have fun and enjoy your time. (This activity should, in itself, be FUN!)

I really enjoy:

- _____

- _____

- _____

- _____

- _____

- _____

Now that you have your list, you can compare it to the one in which you identified how you *waste* time. They should be different lists. (If they're not, then you *really* need to find some ways to have fun that aren't a waste of your time.)

When you do spend time doing something you enjoy, you are fully engaged with the activity. This means that you are fully in the moment and thinking to yourself something along the lines of, "I am enjoying this! It is fun! I am happy doing it! It is the only thing I want to be doing right now! I am glad I am taking the time to do it! I will be really happy that I did it once it's over." Any and/or all of those may pop into your head during the activity, or, as we psychologists say, into your subconscious at least. Meaning, you will have a *sense* that you are having a good time, and equally as important, you will feel that it was a good use of your time afterward. When you waste time, you feel exactly like you wasted time. When you reflect on what you did, you don't feel a sense of satisfaction. You don't have fun memories, you don't feel you gained anything (physically, socially, personally, academically). It's just time that's gone forever and you know it.

A big part of college (and life in general) needs to be fun and enjoyment. These are the things that balance the work part (but not the work for this workbook, because this is fun work, which is absolutely worth your time!). And my big point is (insert drum roll...) **you need to schedule time for FUN!** Just as much as you need to block out time to read your textbooks, write your papers, and study for your tests, you need to make sure you plan time for you to do the things that you want to do. You MUST find time to have a good time.

Naked Exercise #34

Plan to Pick a Planner

Picking out a planner might not seem like fun (although the *Naked Roommate* planner offers a year of "naked" planning fun), but the right planner can allow you to find time to have more fun. Once you have identified your priorities (and don't forget to add some fun in the mix), now it's time to make a schedule. This is one of the best investments of your time you can make. Creating and revising your schedule once a week can save you hours of wasted time (time that you can use for FUN things, once you get all your other stuff done). And to make a schedule, you need to have a planner (but you already knew that because of the header). So get ready to go from plannerless to fully scheduled in five easy steps.

Step 1: Identify Your Schedule Tool of Choice

_____ Electronic calendar (computer)

_____ Electronic calendar (handheld: iPhone, smartphone)

_____ Paper planner

_____ Paper desk calendar

_____ Wall calendar

Whichever one(s) you choose, you'll want to make sure you can easily access them and make changes regularly if necessary. It doesn't do any good to make a plan that you never see and can't alter as life dictates.

So, do you have your planner of choice with you? If not, now's the time to get it in order to be ready to implement step 2. There's no point in just reading step 2 if you're not going to carry it out. That would just be wasting time, and that's what we're trying to avoid (if you just found a new way to waste time, then go back to exercise #31 and add it to the waste of time list). So, in the best interest of your time, either have your planner in front of you with any writing implement necessary to record information on it, or go do something else productive. Step 2 will be waiting for you when you are ready.

Are you back? OK, let's get started.

Step 2: Gather Your Input
Collect all course syllabi, work schedules, bill payment statements, campus club meeting and special event dates, and the list of things you've promised you would do for your mom, best friend, or religious group.

Step 3: Identify Critical Dates
Assignment due dates, exam dates, important meetings, events you are expected to attend, and your great aunt's birthday. Begin by noting these on your calendar in **bold**, or bright colors, or with lots of arrows pointing to them. These are the things you MUST remember to do, and not just on the day you have to do it, but a period of time beforehand, so that you can be well prepared for whatever it is. (NOTE: there's no space provided for you to do this in the workbook—you're supposed to be doing this in your planner of choice.)

Step 4: Identify Important Timely Obligations

- When you are in class
- When you have club meetings
- When you are at work, in church, at your mom's for dinner
- When you go to the gym
- Other important things you need to do

Before you actually allocate your time, we need to do a little preliminary work. This is the part of the workbook where you need to assess your big "events" (you know, tests, papers, etc.—the things that require *work* to do well; and *work* = *time*) and determine what you need to do in order to prepare for each, and how much time you'll need for that preparation. Now we'll give you some space to work this out.

Event: Exam

Subject: _____

Number of pages to read in textbook/handouts: _____

Number of pages of notes to review: _____

Level of difficulty for me: Low   Med   High

Grade I need to earn on exam to keep/raise my grade to desired level: _____

Estimated amount of time necessary to be well prepared: _____

Due date: _____

* * *

Event: Paper

Topic: _____

Library research required: YES / NO

Number of sources: _____

Time estimated to collect resources: _____

Outline required: YES / NO

Time estimated to develop outline: _____

Number of drafts required: _____

Time estimated to write first draft: _____

Time estimated to rewrite: _____

Time estimated to proofread final paper: _____

Current grade in class: _____

Grade needed to maintain/raise grade to desired level: _____

Due date: _____

You may need more than just one of each, but feel free to use the previous exercise as a template and repeat the exercise for each required event. Notice there is a lot of estimating required, and this can be a challenge. This is why you need to put the potential grade in context. This will help you prioritize the event as well. When you have several exams and/or papers due at or around the same time, you may have to make a choice as to which one(s) get the most of your time and attention.

It never hurts to overestimate the time you will need for each element of preparation. If you are productive and successful, you will simply find yourself with some extra time to enjoy any way you choose.

Once you have estimated the time necessary to complete each step of your preparation, you need to look at the days, or even weeks, leading up to the event. Papers usually require that you begin your work a couple of weeks ahead, while you might be OK with just a week or several days' preparation prior to an exam, depending on how strongly you have mastered the course material and how quickly you can read and *gain something* from it.

Step 5: Determining the Amount of Time You Need

Even if you've answered all the questions in the event assessments, it doesn't tell you how much time to plan for each stage of your preparation. To help you figure out how much time you need, you'll have to do a few more Naked Exercises. Part of this process is to identify your attention span for each task. It is a huge waste of time to sit with a textbook open on your lap for an hour and a half, if you can only focus productively for twenty-five minutes. It is important to be honest with yourself about how long you can realistically engage in a task—reading, writing, looking up books in the card catalog—before your mind drifts off to faraway places. Either read productively or stop and do something else. Pretending to read when nothing is getting into your brain is no better than watching reruns of *The Big Bang Theory* instead of studying (and no, watching *TBBT* does not help when it comes to science courses).

Naked Exercise #35

Knowing Your Limits

Take a few minutes to complete the following sentences:

The optimum amount of time I can read from my _____ textbook in

order to concentrate and learn the material (and not drift off) is _____.

The optimum amount of time I can read from my _____textbook in

order to concentrate and learn the material (and not drift off) is _____.

The optimum amount of time I can read from my _____ textbook in

order to concentrate and learn the material (and not drift off) is _____.

The optimum amount of time I can read from my _____ textbook in

order to concentrate and learn the material (and not drift off) is _____.

The optimum amount of time I can read from my _____ textbook in

order to concentrate and learn the material (and not drift off) is _____.

The optimum amount of time I can read from my _____ textbook in

order to concentrate and learn the material (and not drift off) is _____.

* * *

The optimum amount of time I can review my lecture notes from my _____

class and concentrate enough to learn the material is _____.

The optimum amount of time I can review my lecture notes from my _____

class and concentrate enough to learn the material is _____.

The optimum amount of time I can review my lecture notes from my _____

class and concentrate enough to learn the material is _____ .

The optimum amount of time I can review my lecture notes from my _____

class and concentrate enough to learn the material is _____ .

* * *

The optimum amount of time I can work on writing a paper for my _____

class and produce coherent, meaningful work is _____ .

The optimum amount of time I can work on writing a paper for my _____

class and produce coherent, meaningful work is _____ .

The optimum amount of time I can work on writing a paper for my _____

class and produce coherent, meaningful work is _____ .

* * *

Clearly, not all classes will require the same amount of time or be as interesting to you. One reason is that some classes will be more relevant to you than others. For example, an English major might stay up all night reading Shakespeare while the accounting major can handle about fifteen minutes before thought tunes out.

If you are only able to focus for about twenty-five minutes, schedule your reading sessions for twenty-five minutes. BUT, if you have a lot of reading to do, you may have to schedule several twenty-five-minute periods in a day, over several days. And that's okay. In between reading, you can do something for another class (a very different kind of activity) or something you enjoy (like finding out info on Facebook about that girl or guy sitting next to you in class). If you don't have a lot of prep time for an upcoming exam, you may find your days have four or five reading sessions, interspersed with meal times and a run on the treadmill. Do what you must to refresh your brain, but get your reading done.

Naked Exercise #36

Finding Your Flexibility

Your time belongs to YOU! Your day, your week, your month, it's all yours in college. You have several options when planning your days, weeks, months, and semesters. Prior to big events (exams or paper due dates), see if you can reduce some of your regularly scheduled commitments. Can you miss a club meeting on occasion? Can your friend take a rain check on that standing coffee date? Can your laundry hold out another day? If so, you can open up more time to insert these necessary periods of reading, researching, reviewing, writing, or programming.

Weekly routines that are flexible and can be changed when I need to study or write an upcoming paper:

Monday _____

Tuesday _____

Wednesday _____

Thursday _____

Friday _____

Saturday _____

Sunday _____

Naked Exercise #37

Searching for Hidden Time Treasures

Remember back to Naked Exercise #8 when you added up all the minutes you spend online and talking with friends on your cell phone? No? If not, go back and refresh your memory—it's important.

Here's where I'm going with this. On an average day, there is downtime that can become productive time. There are stolen minutes that can add up to valuable productive time. You might find you can use your time to multitask and make the most of eating or working out. Here are some examples:

- An hour between classes can be a time to stay on campus and find a quiet place to study while you are waiting for your next class.
- Eating alone can give you a chance to read or review notes while dining.
- Arrive at class early and review notes, jot down ideas for your paper, or focus on a single graph or table in a textbook while waiting for the professor to arrive.
- Review notes on the treadmill during your workout.
- Record your notes and play them on your MP3 player while walking, riding your bike, running, climbing the stair machine, or riding the bus.
- Play your audio notes while riding the bus, driving a car, walking to class, shopping for groceries, or sitting in class before it starts.
- Review or read, even for a few minutes, before you turn out the light to go to sleep.

This time management strategy is sometimes called the "swiss cheese" approach (if you're allergic to cheese, you can call it the "hole in the sock" approach), as you fill the many small "holes" of free time during your day with something productive. Of course, it doesn't always have to be studying that you schedule during these brief periods. You could make great use of these times to make your grocery list, jot down phone calls you need to return, update your planner, or make a purposeful effort to relax and breathe deeply.

Time "holes" during my days that I can fill with productive things:

Monday _____

Tuesday _____

Wednesday _____

Thursday _____

Friday _____

Saturday _____

Sunday _____

Naked Exercise #38

Be Ready to Adapt

Ever watch a football game where the quarterback calls an audible?

An audible is when the quarterback changes the play seconds before the play. A player on the field has to be ready to adapt or he will run the wrong play.

No matter how much effort you put into creating your semester, monthly, weekly, or daily schedules—they are likely to change. Professors will call an audible and rearrange due dates and possibly move exams, meetings will get cancelled or added, events will arise, friends and family will need you unexpectedly (or bail out on plans you made). When these things happen, you need to be ready for it. This means that you will always be working to adapt your schedule to the changes that occur around you. Don't take this task lightly! You truly need to rethink your calendar so that you don't end up wasting time when the unexpected pops up.

Consider the unexpected changes in your days over the past week. How did you adapt to the change? Did you make good use of any extra time? Were you able to rearrange your existing schedule to accommodate new demands? Analyze the week and think about what you might do differently in the future.

Unexpected Change in Schedule	How I Spent My Extra Time	What I Rearranged to Gain Extra Time

Looking back, what I would have done differently to better use my time:

_____

_____

_____

Naked Exercise #39

Tune in to Your Rhythms

Some times to study are better times than others. It's all about your biological rhythms. You know...are you a night owl who likes staying up all hours and not taking your first class before noon? Or, are you an early bird who likes to start your day as early as possible and finish all your necessary tasks so that you can have a free evening and get good sleep? Either way, you'll want to capitalize on this to design your optimum schedule. If you can't get up before 8:00 a.m. then don't plan on doing reading at 7:00 a.m. It's not going to happen.

Fill in the best time for you to be the most alert and focused while doing the following:

- Sitting in a lecture-based class, listening, and taking notes _____

- Sitting in a problem-solving, equation-working class _____

- Reading for class _____

- Writing _____

- Being hands-on in lab so as to not blow anything up _____

- Eating: breakfast _____ lunch _____ dinner _____

- Working out _____

- Socializing _____

NOTE: If you are bored by a subject that you are required to take, register for a section that occurs during your most awake and productive times of day. Your interest in a class will help push you through the more difficult times for your biorhythms (for example, the after-lunch-it's-time-for-a-nap slump), but if you don't like the material or the class format is very passive, you must avoid putting yourself in this situation if possible.

This goes for reading, reviewing, writing, and studying for courses as well (you may not have as much say in when you can take a class, but you can definitely arrange your outside-of-class schedule around your optimal times for concentration). Don't plan to read on a full stomach if you get sleepy easily. Don't plan to watch the DVR'd episodes of your favorite show when you are full of energy and have the ability to focus; save it for your downtime. Capitalizing as much as possible on your physical and mental states that vary throughout the day can really optimize your schedule and your ability to stick to it successfully.

Naked Exercise #40

Take Advantage of the "Holes"

Identify times to:

- Go to the library to do research for your paper
- Read your class assignments
- Do your math homework
- Review your notes to prepare for your exam
- Write up your lab report
- Create your outline for your paper
- Write your computer program

You have some good strategies now for finding the time, particularly if you need extra time, during your weeks to prepare for important events. As you look at your semester calendar, begin to block out specific times to engage in your preparatory activities (but remember to be realistic as to how long to spend on each).

And don't procrastinate. While most of us do it, most of us also know that procrastinating is a bad thing. Some people say they work best under pressure, but the truth is, they *hate* the feeling of stress that leads up to their last-minute completion of a task. Believe me, no one is feeling relaxed and in control of his or her life when working on a paper at 2:00 a.m. Then the printer runs out of ink. Don't go there. You will hate it, and the best you will feel is relief when you produce something—anything—to hand in. And even then, you'll probably know that it's crap. And you'll be mad at yourself. You'll feel out of control. Stressed. Then you'll wish you had taken the time to manage your time.

Find Ways to Adapt

For time management, as with everything else in college, you should expect the unexpected. You may work really hard to create a wonderful and effective schedule for your semester, month, or week, when all of a sudden your time needs change. This can happen in a couple of ways—either your professors decide to alter the upcoming test day or day your paper is due, or perhaps you now realize that you need more time than you originally thought to study for the next history exam. Don't panic! There are ways to deal with these new demands in such a way as to give you as much control over your time as you originally had planned. You just need to be purposeful about it.

Take a second to use this space to share your biggest time management challenge that you've faced in the past.

_____

_____

_____

Applying what you've learned so far, what can you do in college to help you break this pattern?

_____

_____

_____

Naked Exercise #41

Time to Write Papers (Big Ones, Small Ones, and In-Between Ones)

One of the most intimidating demands on your time is having to research and write papers. A twenty-page paper might sound intimidating, but if you have twenty-one days to write it, that's less than a page a day (even less if you triple-space your text). Most papers are often assigned with an ample amount of time to do any necessary research, create an outline, and write several drafts. In other words, you can have weeks leading up to a last-minute flurry or crazy overwhelming work.

The biggest misconception is that a research paper is one gigantic task. It's very hard to get motivated to take on something so demanding. But when you discover that the process of writing a paper is just that—a *process* that is made up of many little steps—you will see it in an entirely different light. And this will enable you to schedule it painlessly into your master plan so that you can conquer the "mountain" with steady, well-paced steps.

Step 1: Put Together a Plan

You've just been assigned a research paper (OH NO!). It requires that you choose a specific topic in the area of cognitive development and gather five professional sources and submit it in final form in three weeks. How do you tackle this assignment?

Write each individual step you must take to complete this assignment in full—beginning with selecting a topic and ending with proofreading the final draft. Also indicate how long you will spend on each step.

Steps Toward Paper Completion   Time Allotted

1. _____   _____

2. _____   _____

3. _____   _____

4. _____   _____

5. _____   _____

6. _____   _____

7. _____   _____

8. _____   _____

9. _____   _____

10. _____   _____

Now let's see how your approach matches with a time management plan that allows for you to complete all the necessary steps in a reasonably paced progression.

Step 2: Locate a Librarian (They Can Usually Be Found in a Library)

Sitting in front of a computer in the library and doing hours of research is not most students' first choice when it comes to passing time. It's easy to avoid doing the research, that is, until you realize you've waited too long. Then it's time to panic, rush, and hand in that not-so-good paper.

Here's a hint to help you cut down on your time. Find a librarian to help. Librarians save you time!

Use your library website to identify the resource librarian(s) who can help you with whatever research your project requires. Some libraries have particular librarians assigned to certain disciplines—check to see if this is the case at your institution, or if there are other specific types of librarians available to help you. Once you familiarize yourself with who's who in your library, you will have a much easier time taking that first step to getting started on your research.

Library Resource Staff

Name	Position	Contact Information

Once you've familiarized yourself with the key library staff, make contact as soon as you get your first research-based assignment. The librarian(s) should become one of your BEST friends. The time you invest working with a librarian will save you many hours of searching aimlessly through tens of thousands of books and articles that will leave you frustrated, exhausted, and very possibly no further along than when you started.

Resource librarians will point you in the right direction and give you the know-how to quickly and easily access the sources that will be useful to you. In fact, they like helping. It makes them feel good. Help them by allowing them to help you.

Step 3: Doing Research

While you may have to find several sources for your paper, you don't have to get them all at once. Plan several shorter visits to the library in which you are intensely focused on scouring for books and articles, but where you don't stay so long your vision is blurry and you are tired of your topic before you write the first word. Consider three to five visits of an hour or less, to give you plenty of time to read through abstracts, note potential candidates for your paper, and make the necessary copies to bring home to read.

Time frame: Within the first 7–10 days.

Step 4: Identifying Your Sources

Once you've got your selection of potential sources, you'll need to decide which ones will be ideal for your paper. This means digging in and doing some reading (so you'll need to remember the rule about your optimal time frame for reading). Schedule time in your planner to skim your articles—which means read through them, but "lightly." During this step you only need to look for information that you believe will be ideal for helping you write your paper, not glean the deep philosophical meaning.

Time frame: One or two brief sessions during days 11–13.

Step 5: Reading with a Purpose

Once you have narrowed down your resources to only those you will use for your paper, it's time to read them seriously and take notes to help you plan and write your paper. Reading with a purpose is much easier, as it is an *active* way to read (something you'll hear more about later). With pen and paper close by, get ready to answer some questions.

At this point you should have your topic in mind, as well as what you're looking to get from the sources you've identified. As you do your reading and research, look for the specific information and ideas that you will use to support your main points (or perhaps this reading will help you identify your points). The goal of reading at this point is to begin formulating your points and the outline of your paper—the best order in which to address the issues you will discuss. You'll need to spend a bit more (serious) time with each of your chosen sources at this stage to highlight and take note of the most important elements from each.

Time frame: One highly focused session with each source within days 14–16.

Step 6: Outlining

Think of your paper in terms of a detailed sketch or a blueprint. Once you create the outline or structure, you'll know what you need to fill in the details. Do this and you'll practically have your paper written before you even turn on the computer.

When you create your outline, you'll need headings and subheadings. This is where you can notate which source(s) will be presented in that section. Since you already highlighted and noted these significant passages of information during the previous step, you've already got your key points lined up and ready to write about.

Time frame: One session reviewing notes from the reading and plotting the final outline. Day 17 (or 16 if you are really pleased with your progress from the previous step!).

Step 7: On Your Mark, Get Set, Go Write!

Once you create your outline from your research notes, you're ready to write! At this point, all you really need to do is "connect the dots" of all your big topical points. The headings on the outline form the basis for your main thesis sentences, and your subheadings indicate all your supporting points. Translating the information you gleaned from your research into your own words and mingling them with your own ideas (or whatever the assignment requires you to do) is all that's left! Your first draft should unfold in a breeze.

Time frame: Three to five sessions during days 17–19.

Step 8: Finalizing and Proofreading

Writing from a solid outline and explicit research notes should enable you to produce a first draft that is close to being in final form. You will get a sense of how well it flows as you write the first time around, but if you dig in during those few sessions, you can knock out a good paper on your first try. After you sleep on it, re-read it with a fresh perspective and take another pass at it with your notes close by. Step away once more and have someone else read it. Do a spell check and read it out loud for the final proofing.

Time frame: Two sessions on day 20. Ready to turn in on day 21—three weeks from the assigned date.

The Naked Conclusion

This is just one basic model with a particular (three-week) time frame. You are not likely to have a three-week time frame to write all—if any—of your papers. But, I wanted to give you a sense of how to break down a large, involved project into smaller parts to make it more manageable. This will help guide you as you fill out your semester calendar.

Blocking out enough time (and numerous smaller chunks of time) to complete a paper is important. You shouldn't ever block an entire day or two before the due date to write a paper. You'll stress about it, beat yourself up for doing it that way, and ultimately, you won't get as good a grade. And as you now know, there's a much easier option.

Naked Exercise #42

Protect Your Time

Your time belongs to you. *Be protective of your time.* It is easy to let other people take up your time, whether they mean to or not. The key is that YOU have to make a promise to yourself (yes, more promises) that you will be true to YOUR needs and wants when considering how you use your time.

Of course I'm not advocating that you ignore your sad friend's plea for a shoulder to cry on, or that you refuse to help your mom decorate for Aunt Sophie's ninety-seventh birthday party (don't you just love Aunt Sophie?). But I am telling you that it's very important you don't consistently let others' requests destroy your carefully planned schedule and deprive you of both the study time and fun time you need to be successful in college.

Friends, family, and significant others don't necessarily mean to mess you up in terms of your time, but when they are focused on their needs and wants (from you), they tend to forget you may have your own important things to do. This is where you need to be strong and critically think about what accommodating someone else will require.

The next time someone asks something of you, don't immediately jump at the opportunity. First answer the following questions (you'll need to refer to your planner for this).

How much of your time will it take? _____ (Consider what they are asking for and what the *reality* is likely to be.)

When do they need your time? _____

What does it conflict with (what else did you have planned at that time—use your planner)?

_____

_____

_____

How will you rearrange your schedule to give them this time?

_____

_____

_____

How important is this person to you and why?

_____

_____

_____

Is what you are being asked to do with your time necessary for them and worth it to you? How will you feel afterward? Are you likely to be glad you gave the time or regret that you screwed your entire week's schedule up? Why or why not?

_____

_____

_____

Why is it important to you to consider their request?

_____

_____

_____

What would the consequences be if you told them you were not able to give them the time they're asking for?

_____

_____

_____

You don't have to write anything down every time you encounter an unexpected (and uncomfortable) request for your carefully planned time, but this is a good mental exercise to go through so that you can make sound decisions about the things you do. Helping people close to you who are truly in need is important. Agreeing to do anything for anyone at any time, at your own expense, is not. You need to figure out the demands of each situation and be prepared sometimes to just say no.

Naked Exercise #43

Giving Your Parents "The Talk" about Time

Sometimes, family members will want more of your time than you can give them. This can be *very* hard (especially if Mom and Dad are helping to pay the bills and are used to controlling how you spend your time). But that cannot be the case anymore since you are an independent young adult in charge of managing his or her own time.

Sometimes this is difficult for Mom and Dad to see (or accept), and you will have to help them understand the important demands on your time. We all want this to be a positive process (that's right, Harlan and I care that you maintain a great, loving relationship with your parents, even when you have to teach them some difficult lessons).

So if protecting and managing your time has become difficult with regards to the expectations, wishes, and possibly demands of your parents, plan to have a conversation with them about it. Be gentle. Go easy on them. But protect your time.

Prepare for your conversation with Mom and Dad.

- Bring your planner so that you can show them your busy schedule with all your important and necessary obligations mapped out for the semester.

- Highlight your academic responsibilities first. Show them time spent in class, and all the additional time you've scheduled for reading, researching, writing, and studying.
- Show them your extracurricular schedules. Remind them that campus involvement is important for your leadership development and getting to know important staff and faculty on campus for future letters of recommendation, lab, research, and internship opportunities, and that employers look for involved undergraduates when they are hiring.
- Explain how you need some time for yourself to work out, relax, and reduce your stress so that you stay healthy and happy—which is necessary for you to do well in school, graduate on time, and cost them less money.

If they simply want some regular time with you on the phone or in person, then find a good time for everyone and work it into your weekly schedule. Planning routine visits may alleviate the unexpected requests for your time, or at least it will make it easier for you to decline if you have too much to do. Respect that they are making a transition too, one that may be a bit harder in terms of their own time management, if they counted on you for some regular help with the family routine. Then teach them all you've learned about how to create a great schedule and get the most from the time you have! And of course, feel free to get them a copy of Harlan's book, *The Naked Roommate: For Parents Only* and help them get a better sense of just how demanding life in college can be and what they can do to help.

Penciling in your parents (you can refer back to Naked Exercise #6). Now that you have a better sense of your time commitments and schedule, revisit communicating with your parent. You might need to tweak talk time:

The best day of the week: _____

The best location to talk to your parents: _____

The best way to communicate (text, phone, video chat): _____

How you can explain the best times for you to communicate without hurting anyone's feelings or having financial assistance yanked:

_____

_____

Rate using a scale of 1–10.

> **1 = Not true → 5 = Somewhat true → 10 = Doesn't get any truer**

_____ I never miss class unless I am sick.

_____ I try to get a seat near the front of the class.

_____ I am sometimes late for class because I oversleep or lose track of time.

_____ I can't understand what the professor is saying most of the time.

_____ I sit in the back of the room so I can blend in and be anonymous.

_____ I often ask questions in class.

_____ I like to get to class early so that I can talk to the professor.

_____ I don't go to class when the professor just repeats information from the textbook.

_____ I don't go to class when I understand the material.

_____ I don't go to class when I don't understand the material.

_____ Some classes provide a great opportunity to text with my friends and family.

_____ I usually don't know anyone in my classes.

_____ I always make an effort to get to know some people in my classes.

_____ If I miss class, I don't worry about it. I just make sure I read the book to get the information.

_____ I would never ask a question in class; it's too embarrassing.

_____ I prefer to take notes on my computer.

_____ I have a hard time writing down everything the professor says.

_____ I tune out professors when they go off on tangents or start telling personal stories about something we're talking about in class.

_____ I like when we have guest speakers or a video in class—they're good days to skip!

_____ I think that students who ask a lot of questions and talk to the professors are kissing up to get a good grade.

_____ I frequently text or surf the Internet in class when I shouldn't.

Naked Exercise #44

Classroom Savvy

At the end of the fall semester, I often ask each of my first-year students to write down the most important lessons they've learned during their first few months in college. While I get a variety of answers from the group, there is one constant that stands out, one single lesson learned by almost every student, every year: GO TO CLASS!

They've often learned this lesson the hard way—by not going and suffering the consequences. Skipping class is a freedom that most first-year students are anxious to take advantage of. If the professor doesn't take attendance (which most don't), it's your choice whether to go and endure the hours of dry lecture that await if you go.

We understand that many of you would rather be playing World of Warcraft, or sleeping after your late night of socializing. But if you want to actually continue staying in college and graduate with a degree, you'll need to rethink the importance of going to class.

Given your responses to the Naked Self-Exam, you can learn about your approach to class along a few basic dimensions:

- **Attendance**
- **Preparation**
- **Participation**

When you approach each of these with a good attitude (I know, it can be hard sometimes) and a deliberate plan, you will find that not only are you likely to do better in class, but you are likely to actually enjoy the class more.

So let's start by taking a look at your attitudes about class. More importantly, are the ways in which you *approach* class helping or hindering the experience you have in class? If you often dread going to class and even contemplate skipping, it might have something to do with how you are going in to each class period.

- Is your lack of readiness for the lecture resulting in your feeling lost and confused?

YES / NO

- Are you intimidated to ask questions, but need to know the answers?

YES / NO

- Do you feel like the professor doesn't like you?

YES / NO

- Do you know if he or she even *knows* who you are?

YES / NO

- Do you purposefully sit in a seat to be inconspicuous to the professor or your classmates?

YES / NO

- Do you avoid eye contact with your professor to ensure you don't get called on to answer a question?

YES / NO

- Do you avoid talking to your classmates?

YES / NO

- Have you decided that not showing up to class or not doing well on assignments or exams will somehow "punish" a professor you don't like?

YES / NO

- Do you think that if no one asks questions or participates in discussions that the class will just be over quicker and you'll be out of your misery?

YES / NO

- Are you mostly bored, distracted, and uninterested while in class?

YES / NO

If you answered "yes" to most of these questions—even for just a couple of your classes, we've got some work to do! But have no fear, there are ways to overcome these negatives and create a better experience when you are in class.

Naked Exercise #45

To Go or Not to Go...to Class

Admittedly it's a great feeling to be able to choose for yourself whether or not you go to class. You can do WHATEVER you want in college! But, class attendance is expected or at least strongly suggested for a number of important reasons, all of which are directly related to your success in the class and likelihood of actually finishing your degree.

Yes, it's difficult to endure some classes because of the course content (boring or hard), the professor (boring or really hard to understand), the format (boring or really not your preferred way of learning), the time of day (early, late, during mealtime, or naptime), the length (too short to get anything accomplished, too long to endure with continued concentration), or other reasons that I haven't listed, but you have already thought of. However, what you have to gain by going, or what you have to lose by not going, is significant.

Only you truly know both the good and the bad of going to your classes. But if you are going to get through college successfully, you need to identify your challenges with certain classes in order to find ways to deal with them. Only then will you be able to make the grades you want, both in the individual classes and for your overall GPA. Start now by taking an *honest* (once again) look at the pros and cons of attending and skipping class.

Class: _____

Pros of Attending	Cons of Skipping
_____	_____
_____	_____
_____	_____

Pros of Skipping	Cons of Attending
_____	_____
_____	_____
_____	_____

Class: _____

Pros of Attending	Cons of Skipping
_____	_____
_____	_____

Pros of Skipping	Cons of Attending
_____	_____
_____	_____
_____	_____

Class: _____

Pros of Attending	Cons of Skipping
_____	_____
_____	_____
_____	_____

Pros of Skipping	Cons of Attending
_____	_____
_____	_____
_____	_____

Class: _____

Pros of Attending	Cons of Skipping
_____	_____
_____	_____
_____	_____

Pros of Skipping	Cons of Attending
_____	_____
_____	_____
_____	_____

Class: _____

Pros of Attending	Cons of Skipping
_____	_____
_____	_____
_____	_____

Pros of Skipping	Cons of Attending
_____	_____
_____	_____
_____	_____

You've got good reasons for going and good reasons for not going. You've got problems with going and problems with not going. Now what? Let's keep thinking, and examine more closely each of the categories you just filled out.

Naked Exercise #46

Understanding Why You Should Go to Class (as Opposed to Sleeping In)

You've probably identified some things that reflect important reasons in general to go to class—any class. Expand your thinking from here. Consider how each of these factors directly impacts your success in class.

Pros of Attending	How It Will Help Me Succeed in Class
_____	_____
_____	_____
_____	_____

Class time is just the jumping off point for your learning. What you are realistically able to get out of sitting in a classroom for a few hours a week, relative to what you are expected to learn is minimal. That's why going to class is so important. It provides the following:

- Important information that you will need to know in order to perform well on quizzes, homework, exams, and papers
- Examples of how to work problems, demonstrations of lab techniques, additional illustrations of points made in the textbook or other readings
- Time with the professor that gives you the chance to ask questions, clarify information, and understand what he or she thinks is particularly important for you to gain from the class reading assignments and lecture material
- Time with classmates who may ask questions that help you understand the material better, and who can be resources for better notes and study groups
- Opportunities to hear guest speakers and see videos or hands-on demonstrations of important concepts related to the material

Even if your class doesn't offer the last option, all of the others are valid for any class. Material is presented by an instructor who will grade your evaluations. Others taking the class are in the same position you are and presumably want to earn a good grade as well. These are important things to experience regularly, but you need to do more. And that "more" can make the most difficult classes more bearable, if necessary.

Keep your list in mind at all times. But don't stop there; we need to work out the other issues you've identified with regards to attendance.

Naked Exercise #47

Skip Rope, Not Class

This is the other easy category to focus on. You recognize that there are obvious consequences when you miss class—any class—so now you should reinforce these ideas with specifics. Identify specifically how skipping class will impact your ability to get the grade you want.

Cons of Skipping	How It Will Hinder My Class Grades

Again, this is a powerful list to keep on hand. When you entertain the idea of taking a day off from class, remind yourself the price you may be paying.

Cons of Attending

Let's be honest. The list of cons is based purely on what you *want*, not what you need or should be doing. Perhaps that's a little harsh and not entirely true for every item you listed. BUT, this is the list that is the most superficial and without true substance.

Valid, mature, true reasons that support the idea that you *shouldn't* go to class are few and far between. These lists aren't about the occasional day that you are truly sick, or have an important, unexpected time conflict. They are about your approach to going to class in general. You enrolled in a class, you should attend. Reasons not to attend aren't likely to fly—with your professors, your academic advisor, scholarship benefactor, parents, or Jiminy Cricket.

Naked Exercise #48

Take a Minute to Gripe

We psychologists like to prompt people to "own up" to their actions, to admit the real reason they are doing something, want to do something, or don't want to do something. And here's your chance.

I know you feel there are some negative things related to going to class (it's a waste of time, it confuses you more...I've heard many). But they're rarely valid enough to justify a semester of showing up only for exams or to turn papers in. Usually those students aren't very happy with their grade.

Here's your cathartic opportunity to tell why you just don't want to go to class. Go ahead, get it out of your system. Don't hold back—it will make you feel better to write it down. (Just make sure your sensitive instructors don't see this Naked Exercise.)

Cons of Attending	What I Really Mean by This
_____	_____
_____	_____
_____	_____

Now that you're done, leave these feelings in the past and move on.

Pros of Skipping

While this category holds concern too, there may be a few valuable points to be made by considering what you have listed for this area. It is likely though, that these points are related to the occasional incident or unexpected need to skip class, and do not represent a solid argument that missing class on a regular basis for most of the semester is a stellar idea.

Naked Exercise #49

Solving the Problems That Make You Skip Class

All classes should be built into your weekly routine, so as a general rule skipping them should never be an option. If you need more time for other classes, review your weekly commitments, the ways in which you might be wasting time, or study methods so that you can find *other* times to accomplish those things, without sacrificing time in class (yes, even if it's a class you don't like).

For each of your "good" reasons for skipping class, consider what you feel it is "buying" you, and figure out an alternative solution.

Pros of Skipping	Alternative Solution to the Problem
_____	_____
_____	_____
_____	_____

With your collection of the four perspectives on attending and skipping class, you should now have a more complete picture of good reasons to attend and important reasons not to skip. But perhaps the best strategy is to determine if you're going to struggle with going to a class *before it's too late*. In other words, if you can figure out that attending regularly is going to be a challenge before census day (the day that your name goes on the class roll permanently)—or at least before the drop deadline, you will save yourself a lot of trouble.

Oh, and if you really want to find motivation to attend class, ask your parents to fill out the previous Naked Exercises for you.

Anger Management Box

Feel free to scribble angrily if you're upset that you have to go to class. Let it out...

Naked Exercise #50

What the !a!&% Is a Syllabus?

Think of your syllabus like you think of Google maps (but more involved). A syllabus includes information about assignments, due dates, and your instructors. Get it, read it, and think seriously about what it's telling you (it doesn't actually talk, at least not yet). You should receive a syllabus for every class on the very first day. Some professors will review them with you; others will hand them out and never say another word about them. But you are expected to know their contents fully and adhere to them like a contract.

In a sense, that is what a syllabus is—a contract between the professor and you. He states his expectations, policies, format, grading, schedule of topics, assignment due dates, and other important course information, and you can consider yourself *told*. You then are relieved of asking basic questions about the class like "When is our first test?" "Do we have to write any papers?" "How much does homework count toward our grade?" and "Do you give make-up exams?" Most everything that you could want to know about a class is stated in the syllabus. Read it, pay attention to it, and use it. Because no one expects you to memorize everything in every syllabus from every class, keep your syllabus front and center in your notebook for its respective class.

Like I said, a syllabus is a *tool* to help you navigate through class—from telling you how to contact your professor, to when you have exams, to whether or not you can bring your lunch to class. You actively *use* tools, as they are pointless sitting in the toolbox collecting dust. To give you an idea how important they are, let's take a closer look at yours.

Collect all your syllabi from all of your classes.

Got them all? No?

I'll give you a little more time.

Great! Now get your planner. (If you don't have a planner you need to get one. Yes, it's time!)

For each item on the next page, find the information on each of your course syllabi. Read through it to make sure you didn't overlook something the first time you read it (if you read it) and that you are completely clear as to what your instructor means. In the space provided, note anything unusual for each category and jot down anything you need your professor to clarify.

Critical Syllabus Information

Professor and teaching assistant office location, office hours, and contact information:

_____

_____

_____

Prerequisites required for the course (have you completed them all?):

_____

_____

_____

Corequisites required for the course (are you enrolled in everything you need to be?):

_____

_____

_____

Number of credit hours you will earn for the course:

_____

_____

_____

Type of course requirements (attendance, participation, problem solving, writing, objective or subjective exams, research papers, oral presentations, group projects, out-of-class participation, etc.):

_____

_____

_____

Amount of work required (daily homework, weekly quizzes, numerous/few exams, weekly papers, long-term project, etc.):

_____

_____

_____

Reading requirements (daily, weekly, substantial, few and far between, textbook, journal articles, novels, etc.):

_____

_____

_____

Class format (lecture, seminar with student presentations, discussion, hands-on, guest speakers, etc.):

_____

_____

_____

Grading scale (point values, grade curves, weight of assignments/exams relative to grade):

_____

_____

_____

Grading policies (dropping lowest grades, late assignments, make-up exams, etc.):

_____

_____

_____

Extra-credit opportunities:

_____

_____

_____

Course schedule (class days, assignment due dates, exam dates, final exam day/time, readings assigned per day/week, long-term project deadlines, presentation days, etc.):

_____

_____

_____

Classroom policies (no food/drink; be on time; attendance required; no computers; no cell phones; bring textbooks; participation expected; wear shirts, shoes, pants, etc.):

_____

_____

_____

College/university policies (classroom conduct, grade grievance procedure, students with disabilities, field trips, lab safety, etc.):

_____

_____

_____

What did you discover about your classes? Anything that surprised you? Have you noted all the due dates and exam dates on your planner? Hopefully you didn't gain anything from this exercise because you were already familiar with everything there is to know about your classes. But if you weren't, then you need to establish the habit of doing this on the **first day of every class each semester!** The syllabus can tell you a lot more than just the logistics of class.

Naked Exercise #51

Making Sure It's a Match

Now I want you to take a look at your syllabi, but through a different lens. Look at your syllabi in terms of your personal reaction to each class.

When you read the assignments, are you excited to dive in or are you filled with a sense of dread for the semester ahead? When you look at the course format, are you thrilled that it capitalizes on your love of public speaking or is your stomach in knots because you don't want to have to stand out in class?

Go through your syllabi and write down your reactions—both positive and negative—about all the elements of class. Your goal is to assess your feelings going into the class. Now, assuming you are already *in* the class, that's okay—this will still be useful. Just be honest and give your gut reaction to the nature of the course.

Class: _____

1. The way I feel about the things I will be required to do in this class is:

    _____

    _____

    _____

Course requirements involve things I like to do
and relate to how I prefer to learn.   YES / NO

Course requirements seem very unpleasant and
will be hard for me to endure.   YES / NO

2. The way I feel about the amount of work I will be required to do in this class is:

    _____

    _____

    _____

The workload seems reasonable and involves things I like to do.   YES / NO

The workload seems very heavy and may cause problems for me.   YES / NO

3. The way I feel about the type and the amount of reading I will be expected to do in this class is:

_____

_____

_____

The amount of reading seems doable and realistic for me.   YES / NO

I am intimidated by the amount of reading and will likely fall behind.   YES / NO

4. The way I feel about the way the class will be taught on a daily basis is:

_____

_____

_____

I think I will enjoy going to class.   YES / NO

I am concerned that I will not like sitting in class
and may tend to skip.   YES / NO

5. My reaction to where grades come from and how they are calculated is:

_____

_____

_____

The grading system seems fair and realistic. I believe I will do well.   YES / NO

The grading system seems stacked against students and
may be problematic.   YES / NO

6. Looking at the course schedule, I feel:

_____

_____

_____

I believe this class will fit well with the current demands of my life.　　YES / NO

I think I may struggle with this class given the
schedule of expectations.　　YES / NO

7. My reaction to the classroom policies is:

_____

_____

_____

I think the professor is fair and has reasonable
expectations of students.　　YES / NO

I think the policies are limiting and will
cause me to skip class often.　　YES / NO

Overall, I believe this class will be a good fit
for me and I will succeed.　　YES / NO

Overall, I think I will struggle with this class,
not attend, and possibly fail.　　YES / NO

Again, it may be too late in the semester to remedy the situation if you discovered that you have some classes that are not a good fit for you. But if you take the time to think through these things for every class at the beginning of every semester, you may save yourself some big challenges and poor grades. Use your syllabi to get a good, specific look at what you are getting into from Day 1.

Of course, there will always be those classes that you just *have* to take, and the difficult professor whom you *have* to endure, as there are no other options and they are required for your degree. And really, taking a class that forces you to step outside your comfort zone can become one of the very best classes.

Should you find yourself in a classroom situation where you struggle with the requirements, amount of work, grading scheme, and daily format, finding it hard to sit through, there are several things that you can do to meet the challenge. The rest of this section will help you make the best of life in the classroom—whether or not it's a love connection.

Naked Exercise #52

Managing the Mountain of Reading

Approach textbooks and reading like you approach an all-you-can-eat buffet in the dining hall. Instead of feeling overwhelmed and leaving with too much on your plate, walk in with a plan of how you'll approach what seems like a mountain of work. Arrive with a plan and you can avoid wasting valuable time (and food). And feeling sick to your stomach.

Some reading material is central to a course. Other reading materials are not. Some professors repeat the reading material almost verbatim (begging the question, "Why do I need to go to class if I can just read the book—I don't get anything else from being there?" I'll answer that in a minute.). Other professors present material that may seem completely removed from what you read in the text or handouts. Whichever scenario you face, both listening to the lecture and reading the assignments is important. The order in which you do them is up to you, but pay attention to which is more beneficial. Here are some helpful hints:

1. If the textbook is fairly "reader friendly," but your professor is not a great lecturer (hard to follow, difficult to understand, monotone, tends to go off on tangents) read the related assignment BEFORE going to class. It will give you a foundation upon which to interpret the lecture. Even if you think that the lecture and the reading are completely unrelated, you may be surprised if you actually read the material first. Often new connections will be discovered from your prepared framework for listening. I know this is a lot to ask given your busy life on campus, but try it.

2. If you have a professor who presents the material clearly and is pretty easy to follow in class, but the book is somewhat challenging, don't take on the reading until after the lecture. BUT, read the assignment relatively soon after class. This will help you get more from the reading.

3. If you have a professor who repeats the material from the text directly, take the opportunity to use this "doubling up" of exposure to the information to study more easily for the test. Do the reading, listen to the lecture, and this duplication of information will help you learn it quickly and without as much heavy-duty studying. But you have to commit to doing both to make it work. Don't skip class, don't ignore the reading. And use class time to ask questions. This is the best chance to fully understand the material since the lecture and reading cover the same information. If you don't understand something in the book, having read the material ahead of time, you can ask very specific questions in class and get an answer. Take advantage of this opportunity to really master a smaller set of concepts.

Given the important combination of reading and listening to lectures in class (or attending lab), determine the best order for your approach to doing both in each of your classes. Write the class name and check the line that fits best:

Class: _____ Read first: _____ Attend lecture first: _____

Class: _____ Read first: _____ Attend lecture first: _____

Class: _____ Read first: _____ Attend lecture first: _____

Class: _____ Read first: _____ Attend lecture first: _____

Class: _____ Read first: _____ Attend lecture first: _____

Class: _____ Read first: _____ Attend lecture first: _____

Now try out your plan, and don't forget to consider this when you are creating your schedule in your planner!

Naked Exercise #53

The Power of Questions

We professors *looooovvvve* when students ask questions! It shows us that you are listening to us in class, it shows that you are reading the material, and it shows that you are thinking about the topic. ASK LOTS OF QUESTIONS! Because you will get a lot out of it too, perhaps in more ways than you think.

Asking questions gets you much more than just answers. Consider the following:

- Asking questions gives you the answers to things you don't know that might be on the test (OK, that's the one you expected).
- Asking questions gives you an active way to approach reading your textbook and reviewing your notes when studying. When you break up sitting and staring at the words by writing down questions for your professors, you will be more engaged with the material.
- Asking questions gives you an active way to approach class, and this can be a big help when you have a dull, monotonous professor. When you ask a question, the class gets to hear someone else's voice (yours) and maybe the professor will even step away from his old yellowed notes for a moment and say something different.
- Asking questions will inspire others in your class to ask questions. This may help *you* understand the material better (you may discover there are things you didn't know you didn't know—until someone asks the right question). And all this question-asking may really energize the professor. (And when others ask questions, you can see who in your class might be a good study partner or source of notes if you must miss class because you're sick.)
- Asking questions can get you more comfortable with the professor. Once you aren't hesitant to approach her, you will more easily seek out her help during office hours to optimize your chance of getting a good grade in class. In fact, approaching a professor with a question about class material is a good ice-breaker if you want to talk to her about other things like a chance to work in her lab, do an independent study, learn about careers in your major, or build a relationship for a future letter of recommendation.
- Asking questions can get the professor to know you. He will also think you are a good student who reads and listens and wants to do well in class. And he will keep that in mind when he is grading your tests and papers.

So, if asking questions is so important, why is it that so many students don't ask questions? List ten reasons you DO NOT ask questions when you have them. (If you ALWAYS ask questions, come up with ten reasons why other students don't ask questions):

1. _____

2. _____

3. _____

4. _____

5. _____

6. _____

7. _____

8. _____

9. _____

10. _____

Now, for all the reasons you listed above, list a way you can approach the situation so you can ask the question and get the information you desire. For example, if one of the reasons you listed is that you don't want to look stupid, reframe it. You're not going to look stupid, you're going to look like you're hungry for information. Give your instructor a chance to do what he or she loves to do—teach someone who is eager to learn.

Take five items from the previous list and reframe them so nothing can deter you from asking questions that will help you learn.

1. _____

_____

2. _____

_____

3. _____

_____

4. _____

_____

5. _____

_____

Naked Exercise #54

Ask Questions in Class (in Front of Everyone)

Chances are you will have questions related to material in each of your classes. It's IMPOSSIBLE to NEVER have questions. C'mon, I know you aren't clear on everything in the book and from your lecture notes. Get in the habit of acknowledging your questions. Write them down when they come to you (while reading or during class) and get in the habit of *asking* them. Here's your chance to start and get all those pent-up questions out in the open.

Get your textbook or lecture notes out, review them, and put your questions here. Or better yet, jot them in your class notebook so you'll have them with you in class. But if you prefer to put them here, we're happy to provide you that option. And you can conveniently tear out this page and bring it to class with you.

Class: _____

Questions for my instructor or study group:

_____

_____

_____

Class: _____

Questions for my instructor or study group:

_____

_____

_____

Class: _____

Questions for my instructor or study group:

_____

_____

_____

Class: _____

Questions for my instructor or study group:

_____

_____

_____

Naked Exercise #55

Participation = "Points"

Assuming you attend class, you will be able to participate. Participation means a lot of things in this context, but the most basic definition is that you are engaged with the class. And that begins the moment the professor enters the room.

Here's some inside info that will help you (don't tell anyone I told you). There are things that I refer to as the "subtleties of participation" that many first-year students don't know. Once you learn them, you will both save yourself possible embarrassment and set yourself up as a professor's favorite. You won't know it, but they are giving students "mental points" (or actual points) for many of these subtleties. Consider the following:

- **Read or review ahead.** When you have a framework for the lecture, discussion, or lab demonstration to come, the class time will be so much more beneficial and satisfying. Even if you don't read the new chapter prior to the material, having read the text based on the last lecture's material or having reviewed your class notes will put you in a good position to feel in control of what's to come. You will approach class time much more positively this way.
- **Be on time.** When you walk in (or dash in) late, the professor notices and doesn't like it. Or you. It's rude. You disrupt the professors, disrupt your classmates, and it makes you look irresponsible and self-centered. Waltzing in whenever you feel like it with no regard for anyone else is not how to earn points. It's the way to lose them. It's all downhill from there (umm, I feel strongly about this one).
- BUT YES, there are valid reasons for being late. Just be sure to speak to your professor after class to explain the situation. And when you do arrive late, enter as quietly and unobtrusively as possible. If you must be late on a regular basis, due to having a lab across campus or another professor who dismisses you late, speak with your professor to alert him or her to your situation.
- **Come prepared.** Always have your notebook and something to write with, along with your textbook (if necessary) or any other materials you may need. Not having what it takes to function in class without having to ask someone to borrow something is frustrating and distracts you from what's going on in class.
- **Ask questions.** Asking questions gives you answers and a better understanding of the material. It also shows you are trying and want to learn.
- **Answer questions.** When your professor offers up questions to the group, be the one to take them on. You'll gain the respect of your professor and the appreciation of your classmates (who were relieved they didn't have to answer!).

- **Sit near the front.** It can make a dramatic difference. Let's start with the obvious—sitting in the front of class makes it harder to text, talk to friends, shop online, and sleep. You will also see better, hear better, and appear to be a better student to the professor.

You will ask more questions if you sit near the front because you will feel more like you are talking directly to the professor (and you won't have to look at the sea of faces turning around to look at you in the back of the room). You will be more likely to chat with your professor before or after class—about course materials, expectations, exams, or college in general. It will make you memorable in a positive way.

You will feel like you have a closer relationship sitting closer to your instructor. Your professor will feel closer to you. From your regular attendance, insightful questions, thoughtful answers, and more engaging "presence" (from eye contact, nodding, smiling, active note taking), your professor will get to know you as a student who cares and puts effort into her class. This will matter later on.

What you can take away is that YOU play a huge role in your own classroom experience. It's easy to take a back-row seat, but that's not going to help you thrive in the classroom.

Think about your favorite or most memorable class in high school.

1. How many students were in the class? _____

2. How often did the class meet? _____

3. What did you love about the class?

   _____

   _____

4. Where did you sit?

   _____

5. What were ways you contributed to class? What role did you play in making the class one of the best and most memorable?

   _____

   _____

Take these experiences and bring them to your college classrooms, and you will be one step closer to making that class great.

Naked Exercise #56

Approaching Class with Class

Now that you know the secrets to success, think about your approach to life in the classroom. I particularly want you to consider those classes that you find hard to endure—the ones you want to skip. These are the ones that can kill your GPA.

Write a brief response about your personal approach for each item, and identify how your response might differ for different classes. As you fill this out, try to figure out ways that you can make class a better experience for your own enjoyment.

Are you always on time to class? If not, why not?

_____

_____

_____

How does arriving late affect your time spent in class?

_____

_____

_____

When you read ahead and go into a lecture prepared, does it make a difference in your class experience? Explain.

_____

_____

_____

Where do you sit in each class?

_____

_____

_____

How do you think where you sit impacts your experience in each class?

_____

_____

_____

Which classes do you ask questions and actively participate in?

_____

_____

_____

What enables you to be comfortable doing so in these classes?

_____

_____

_____

What keeps you from participating to this extent in your other classes?

_____

_____

_____

What can you do to help yourself overcome these limitations?

_____

_____

_____

What will you gain by doing so?

_____

_____

_____

In what classes does the professor know your name?

_____

_____

_____

How does this contribute to your experience in the class?

_____

_____

_____

What do you think instructors think about students who consistently arrive late?

_____

_____

_____

What steps might you take to help all of your professors know you?

_____

_____

_____

Might you be doing anything to give your professors a negative perception of you (whether or not they know your name)?

_____

_____

_____

What can you do to remedy this as soon as possible?

_____

_____

_____

How important is having a positive relationship with your professor to your enjoyment of a class? Explain.

_____

_____

_____

I want you to really think about the answer to this last question. Were you even able to answer it? Do you have a positive relationship with any of your professors? Maybe I should first ask if you even have what could be called a *relationship* with any of your professors? If you are wondering what I mean by this, you're going to want to tune in to this next section.

Naked Exercise #57

Dining with Doctors (aka How to Get Your Professor to Take You Out to Dinner)

What? You don't want to go to dinner with your professors? How about lunch? Maybe breakfast? Okay, a light snack? If you're still not interested in breaking bread with a prof, you might want to rethink this. Not only can instructors be very interesting people with lots of cool stories and a little wisdom to share (yes, I have some cool stories and a little wisdom to share), they can also help you reach your academic, career, and even personal goals. (Plus, they also usually know the best restaurants and are likely to pay.)

Before I share more about how extremely valuable it is to get to know your professors, consider how well you know them already. Fill in as much information as you can for each of your current course professors.

Class: _____

Professor's name: _____

Highest level of education: Bachelor's Master's MBA PhD PsyD EdD MD DDS

Undergraduate school: _____ Graduate school: _____

Undergraduate major: _____ Graduate degree: _____

Current position on campus: _____

Number of years teaching at your school: _____ Previous colleges: _____

Area of research: _____

Hobbies: _____

Family (including pets): _____

Other interesting facts: _____

* * *

Class: _____

Professor's name: _____

Highest level of education: Bachelor's Master's MBA PhD PsyD EdD MD DDS

Undergraduate school: _____ Graduate school: _____

Undergraduate major: _____ Graduate degree: _____

Current position on campus: _____

Number of years teaching at your school: _____ Previous colleges: _____

Area of research: _____

Hobbies: _____

Family (including pets): _____

Other interesting facts: _____

* * *

Class: _____

Professor's name: _____

Highest level of education: Bachelor's Master's MBA PhD PsyD EdD MD DDS

Undergraduate school: _____ Graduate school: _____

Undergraduate major: _____ Graduate degree: _____

Current position on campus: _____

Number of years teaching at your school: _____ Previous colleges: _____

Area of research: _____

Hobbies: _____

Family (including pets): _____

Other interesting facts: _____

* * *

Class: _____

Professor's name: _____

Highest level of education: Bachelor's Master's MBA PhD PsyD EdD MD DDS

Undergraduate school: _____ Graduate school: _____

Undergraduate major: _____ Graduate degree: _____

Current position on campus: _____

Number of years teaching at your school: _____ Previous colleges: _____

Area of research: _____

Hobbies: _____

Family (including pets): _____

Other interesting facts: _____

How well did you do?
Were you able to complete most of the information for everyone?
Were you able to complete more than just the name on any of them?
Did you even get all the names right?

If you think that getting to know your professors is silly or a waste of time, you are so wrong. It's not about becoming buddy-buddy with your instructors, but rather it's about paving your own way for success now and in the future for the things you want to do. And it has nothing to do with kissing up. This is about being a willing participant in building relationships with some of the most passionate people you'll meet on campus.

Things You Might (or, um, Should) Know to Build Good Relationships with Your Professors

1. **Your professor's name.** You should at least be able to recognize his or her full name because there may be a lot of Dr. Teachalots out there, but only one Lova Learnalot Teachalot (your professor) who is an expert in the field of Onomatology. When you are writing papers and doing research in the area, you will want to know that all the book and journal article references to L.L. Teachalot are to none other than *your* Dr. Teachalot. And if you are doing the research for her class, you had better know it. Plus, it's just not polite to not know someone's name.

2. **Your professor's highest level of education.** Until you know for certain what degree your professors have, ALWAYS begin by addressing them by "Dr. Teachalot" or "Professor Teachalot." NEVER start out by getting your professor's attention saying Mr., Mrs., Ms., Miss, or especially, "Hey Teach Me Lots" or "T-Dude." This is guaranteed to get you and the dude off to a bad start. Many college instructors have a PhD (a Master's is often required as the minimum degree necessary to teach at a university). These folks have worked very hard for their title and expect students to show the respect that goes along with it. Some are more insistent about it than others, so if they prefer that you call them something else, they'll tell you. Stick with professor or Dr. until otherwise informed.

3. **Your professor's field(s) of study.** Know your professor's area of expertise, which may or may not be the class you are taking with her. Sometimes a professor who is a philosopher may be asked to teach a world religions course. She's likely to be very qualified, but it isn't her main area of focus. Knowing her background might make the class more interesting (world religions taught from a philosophical perspective) or simply enable you to learn more career options for people who major in philosophy.

4. **Your professor is a real person who wants you to be successful.** More times than I can count, students have either told me or written in a paper that they begin college very intimidated by professors. They don't see us as *real people*. A student once wrote: "I discovered they weren't these powerful gods that lord over us and control our lives." Wow, I didn't realize I could have that effect on people. Actually, I don't think that *I* ever did. The perception just comes from an unfamiliarity with people called "professors," and who have an incredibly advanced degree.

The more you discover about your professor as a person, the more you will

- relax around him or her
- possibly enjoy him or her in the classroom, or at least be more understanding about his or her shortcomings as a teacher
- feel you can, and have the right to, approach her and talk to her in person—to ask questions, share concerns, inquire about majoring in the same field, or ask for help in any number of areas

And the more personal things you discover about your professors, the more they will become meaningful to you. And this matters.

Naked Exercise #58

Professing What You Want from Your Profs

What do you want from your professors (other than an A)?

What do you *need* from them? What can they specifically do to help you succeed? Think about it. Write it down. Don't limit yourself to what you can envision. Put your *ideal* out there—what would you really like your professors to do for you?

Copy these pages and answer the following for each professor you have.

Class: _____

Professor: _____

How this professor can help me do better in his/her class right now:

_____

_____

_____

How this professor can help me with problems in another class:

_____

_____

_____

How this professor can help me understand more/decide about my major:

_____

_____

_____

How this professor can help me achieve other academic goals (e.g., get better grades, pass my prerequisites, conduct research, earn a prestigious scholarship, become a T.A.):

_____

_____

_____

How this professor can help me achieve my personal goals (e.g., gain student leadership experience, study abroad, get elected to student government):

_____

_____

_____

How this professor can help me achieve my future career goals (e.g., gain an internship, get into medical school, score an interview with my ideal company):

_____

_____

_____

Keep in mind, you don't even have to have a particular professor for a class in order to get to know him or her.

Naked Exercise #59

Office Hours Awareness

If you can't get to know your professor in class, there's another option—office hours! All professors are required to hold at least a few office hours per week. This is dedicated time set aside to have their doors open and for them to be available for students to come by and talk with them.

All office hours should be stated on the syllabus (along with your professor's office location, phone number, email address, etc.). If you have completely ignored all of this critical information, it's time to pay attention—it may be one of the best things you do for yourself.

Gather up your syllabi and complete the following. Then you can remove the page and place it on the inside front cover of your notebook, or better yet, your planner, so that you can be ready to use it at any time. Make sure to note if they prefer you make an appointment beforehand.

Class: _____   Professor: _____

Office location: _____   Office hours: _____

Phone number: _____   Email address: _____

Appointment preferred: YES / NO

* * *

Class: _____   Professor: _____

Office location: _____   Office hours: _____

Phone number: _____   Email address: _____

Appointment preferred: YES / NO

* * *

Class: _____   Professor: _____

Office location: _____ Office hours: _____

Phone number: _____ Email address: _____

Appointment preferred: YES / NO

* * *

Class: _____ Professor: _____

Office location: _____ Office hours: _____

Phone number: _____ Email address: _____

Appointment preferred: YES / NO

* * *

Class: _____ Professor: _____

Office location: _____ Office hours: _____

Phone number: _____ Email address: _____

Appointment preferred: YES / NO

Prepping for Office Hours

You've found Dr. Harlannah's office. She's there and available to meet with you... now what?

I recommend going into a meeting with your professors with a few specific questions in mind (or on paper if you want to look a bit more official). Following are some questions to consider:

- **Questions about course material:** "I don't quite understand the concept of..." or "Can you please provide additional examples of..."
- **Questions about a quiz, exam, or paper:** "Can you explain what you were looking for in this answer?" or "How could I have written this section better?"

- **Questions about how to prepare for future exams:** "What should I spend most of my time on?" or "Do you recommend a particular strategy for learning this topic?"
- **Questions about your major (presumably for discussions with professors in your field):** "What classes do you recommend I take sooner rather than later?" or "What would be my best course of action if I want a career in this?"
- **Questions about related opportunities:** "I know I'm just a freshman, but do you recommend that I join this organization?" or "What are the benefits of doing research if I want to go into this particular field?"

Questions demonstrate your interest in doing well in your professor's class, as well as showing that you value his or her expertise and knowledge in the field. Questions DO NOT mean you're stupid or uneducated. With concrete questions, you can get real answers (that you may or may not need), but it also enables you to open the door to learn more and go farther.

By the way, I always question students who say they don't have *any* questions about the course material. Until you make all perfect scores on your quizzes and exams, I won't believe you. But my issues aside, if you really can't think of an area you need help on, then simply create a few good, course-material-based questions (that you already believe you know the answers to) just to get the ball rolling. Of course, if you go beyond the basics of the lecture material and ask the professor to expand on things to satisfy your own curiosity, you will not only have a great way to start a conversation, but you will really impress him as well. Consider asking your professor about other classes in the department, academic clubs and organizations on campus, or scholarship opportunities. You can also ask a professor about his or her college experience. Instructors, like most people, love to talk about themselves.

It's time to take the first step: develop a couple of questions to take to each professor to start a conversation. Begin by considering if you really do have course content-related information that you would like clarified, or things you want to know about how to do better on your next exam. But beyond that, see if you can find some interest aspects of the class or your career ideas to ask your professors about. This is the real thing. Make it work for YOU.

Class: _____

Professor: _____

Course content questions:

_____

_____

_____

Major/career related questions:

_____

_____

_____

* * *

Class: _____

Professor: _____

Course content questions:

_____

_____

_____

Major/career related questions:

_____

_____

_____

* * *

Class: _____

Professor: _____

Course content questions:

_____

_____

_____

Major/career related questions:

_____

_____

_____

* * *

Class: _____

Professor: _____

Course content questions:

_____

_____

_____

Major/career related questions:

_____

_____

_____

* * *

Class: _____

Professor: _____

Course content questions:

_____

_____

_____

Major/career related questions:

_____

_____

_____

Now you've got what it takes to make your first visit to your professors' office hours.

Naked Exercise #60

Office Hours Observations

As you sit and discuss your questions with your professor, subtly look around his or her office. (Don't be so obvious that it looks like you aren't paying attention or that you're casing the place.) Do you see pictures of his family or pets? Are there unusual artifacts from exotic places around the world? Do you see a diploma hanging on the wall? How about a rainbow indicating he's an ally? Are there political buttons or movie posters? Do you see pictures of your professor skiing, playing trombone, or running in a marathon? All these items tell a story. Take mental notes of what you are seeing and consider what it tells you about him or her. This will help you take the next step in getting to know your professors.

List five things you observed in your professor's office:

1. _____

2. _____

3. _____

4. _____

5. _____

Did you list anything that indicates you have something in common with your instructor (you have a labradoodle puppy, you water ski, you've always wanted to go to Greece, or you are a big fan of Marlon Brando). Professors decorate their office with these various items to show them off to people! Each item has meaning and tells a story. If your instructor didn't want you to know about her political leanings or latest vacation destination or favorite movie, she wouldn't prominently display evidence for all to see. These are great conversation starters that take you beyond course material and into the realm of...the *personal*!

Once you address all your course questions, determine if your professor is in a hurry to get back to his or her work, or if there are other students waiting for their turn in the office. If it appears like there are no pressing matters for your professor, consider asking some other questions about the things in his or her office you observed.

It is often these displays of personal items—professors' likes, experiences, life beyond the classroom—that open students' eyes to the fact that we are "human." Professors are real people with real (regular) lives (except that we've gone to school *a lot* longer, and are older, and know more in general). But beyond that—you and I may have a good deal in common, and that makes for enjoyable conversation and a personal connection.

If you don't get the chance to comment about something you notice on the first visit, there will be other opportunities. Go up to your professors after class and say that you remember seeing something in their office about...You found it really interesting because you also like...If it's something they're interested in, they will enjoy talking about it with you.

What's the Point of Taking an Interest in Your Professor's Life?

Whether the point is to get help in class right now, guidance for future class scheduling, or help with making connections in the business world, the more you get to know your teachers—**and the more you allow them to get to know you**—the easier it will be to get their assistance in all the ways you'd like. Unlike high school, you need to make the effort. It's not that professors don't want to know you, but the dynamics of college make it harder for them to get to know you.

Professors' jobs include teaching, sometimes conducting research, sitting on various campus committees, and *helping students*. True, not all are as equally open and accommodating, but most want to help students achieve success.

Yes, professors are interesting people and getting to know them will make your life inside the classroom so much better. But there's an added bonus.

Professors are ultimately asked to determine what kind of student you are, and this is represented in your letter grade at the end of the semester. Recall that A = Outstanding, B = Above Average, C = Average, D = Below Average, and F = Failing. Many things determine the type of student that you are, beyond how well you perform on tests. Now, I must state the disclaimer that grades are fundamentally based on fair grading practices and primarily reflect your mastery of the course content. But there is more—and it's important.

Some grading is of a subjective nature (short answer, essay questions on an exam, a paper, or written homework assignment), and I have to make judgment calls. These "judgments" are about your degree of understanding of the material—and if you haven't presented that 100 percent accurately and perfectly clearly in your writing, I have to make my best guess. How do I do this? I reflect on what I know about you:

- Do I know who you are (can I picture your face when I read your name on the exam)?
- Are you in class regularly?
- Do you come on time?
- Do you ask relevant questions that show me you came prepared for class and are listening to my lecture?
- Do you volunteer to answer questions I ask to the class, showing me that you are engaged in the material?
- Do you participate in class discussions, indicating that you find the topic interesting and have thought critically about it?
- Have you taken advantage of my office hours to ask further questions, clarify what you don't understand, and give yourself the best opportunity to do well on the assignments and exams?
- Have you shared your academic goals with me so that I know you are serious about doing well and graduating in good standing?
- Have you demonstrated that you are willing to give the time and energy to do what it takes to be successful?

When I can reflect on students in these ways and I have a more complete picture of *you as a student*, I can be more confident that you are learning the material in class, and with less-than-ideal answers, I am willing to give you the benefit of the doubt. Again, I'm not promising this in all situations for all professors, but showing professors that you are invested in your education (starting with your performance in their class) will open many doors for you.

And that dinner, lunch, breakfast, or snack? What an interesting, exciting, and valuable way to spend an evening. Good food and engaging conversation with people who know so much, have unique life experiences, and who can provide solid insight to help you go far. If your professor doesn't ask first—you should. (But let him or her pick the restaurant!)

Rate using a scale of 1–10.

> **1 = Not true → 5 = Somewhat true → 10 = Doesn't get any truer**

_____ I'm excited for this section of the workbook!

_____ I can't read my own handwriting.

_____ I try to write down everything the professor says during lecture.

_____ I am relieved when the professor goes off on a tangent or tells personal stories so that I can take a break from writing notes!

_____ I prefer to take notes on my computer or tablet.

_____ I take notes, but never look at them again.

_____ I use the Cornell Note-Taking Method.

_____ I tend to miss class a lot, but I get other people's notes.

_____ I never really know what I should be writing down.

_____ I prefer to just listen to the professor rather than trying to listen and write at the same time.

_____ I doodle a lot in my class notes.

_____ I like to rewrite or retype my notes after class.

_____ My notes are useless for studying.

_____ I take notes when I read the textbook.

_____ I can't write fast enough to get everything down in my notes.

_____ I like it when the professor has a PowerPoint presentation that I can copy from during lecture.

Naked Exercise #61

A Note-Taking Dance Party

Get ready for nonstop excitement. This is the part of the workbook that you've been waiting for! Not really...

No matter what kind of class (except maybe dance or wine tasting) you are likely to need to record information presented by the professor so that you can refer to it in the future in order to solve problems, balance equations, write a paper, or pass an exam. So taking notes is important. I'm here to help you to become a top-notch note-taker.

If you'd like to make this note-taking section more exciting, feel free to make it a note-taking dance party. The way you do this is put on the top-ten songs of the week via a countdown (get a podcast) and dance while you read.

Before diving into this section, put together your playlist of music (yes, I'm serious). I want to make this note-taking section rock.

Playlist for note-taking section—top ten songs to play:

1. _____

2. _____

3. _____

4. _____

5. _____

6. _____

7. _____

8. _____

9. _____

10. _____

Naked Exercise #62

A Different Kind of Writing Test

The Note-Taking Basics

How do you take your coffee? One cream? Two sweeteners? Just black? You don't drink coffee? OK, how about your tea? Wait, you can't hear me because the music is playing too loud? Turn it down for second or turn it off.

Note taking is like coffee. Everyone has a different taste and preference.

How do you like to take notes? Have you ever thought about it? Are you a fast typist who uses his keyboard every chance he gets or do you like to do it the old-fashioned way with a pen and a clean sheet of college-ruled notebook paper? Take note that you should take notes the way that works best for you. The more you struggle (or simply hate) the method, the less effective you will be at recording the information you need.

If you prefer to take notes on your laptop, **ask your professor's permission** (check your syllabus first). Many professors are suspicious of students with laptops in class. They may think you are playing video games, shopping, or cruising on Facebook instead of taking notes. Let him or her know your preference, and take a seat near the front so that you can use your computer but also be personally engaged with what the professor is presenting. And don't forget to hit SAVE a lot. (NOTE: my computer just crashed and I had to rewrite this.)

If you prefer the traditional method of writing—with paper and pen—take the time to make sure you've got your favorite kind of pen or pencil with you each day for class and lots of fresh paper. Spend that extra fifty cents to get the pen with the rubber guard. Make an investment in your note-taking tools. It's one of the most important things you will do for your education.

Don't have a favorite type of pen? You are missing out! Tear out this page and take it to your campus bookstore's pen section. Use this space to test out all kinds and colors of pens until you find one that you love. What does "loving" a pen mean? Well, basically that it's comfortable to hold, you like how it feels when you write with it, and it makes your handwriting look awesome! Or at least legible.

Also pick a color that you can read easily (and this depends on the color of paper you are using too—white or legal pad yellow, for example). You want a result that draws you back, not turns you off reading what you've written.

Test pens here:

Name of favorite pen (so you'll remember what to buy in the future):

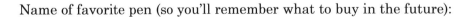

If you prefer to type your notes, that's OK. But you're missing out on all the pen action and excitement.

Naked Exercise #63

Organizing Notes So You Can Use Them

Taking notes is a helpful start. But being able to use them (and read them) is even better.

Think of your class notes as a tool. A tool that you use to guide you when you need to solve math problems (outside of class), remember how to balance chemical equations (outside of class), label maps, identify body parts, and learn lots of detailed information about lots of subjects. Just like the tools made from stainless steel and wood, you need to know which ones to use when and for what task. And you need to know where to find them.

Organizing your notes simply means that you should have notebooks that have separate sections for each course, and daily notes should be clearly dated, labeled, and kept in order. The paper and binders you select to keep your notes in should be designed so that you can easily locate your notes for each class, and should be practical to carry around with you throughout each class day.

Heading each page of notes with the date they were taken, the chapter the lecture relates to (if possible), and any other useful labels will cause you to thank yourself later when you go back to review them. Don't waste your time having to search for notes or trying to figure out which order your pages go in.

If you take notes on your computer, create separate file folders for each course and label your files with the class name and date for easy retrieval.

> **Hey, how's that dance party going? Getting tired? Take a break and cool down. The note-taking party will be here when you get back!**

Format Format Format

Back to note taking...How you translate information from a lecture or a book into your own notes is a highly personal thing (and don't let anyone tell you otherwise!). What you write down and how you write it should reflect *your* understanding of the material, in the order in which you will be able to make the necessary connections later, and with all of the visual cues you believe are important for helping you remember the information when you go back to study it.

Having said that, not everyone has a specific or deliberate approach to taking down information. This can make reviewing notes difficult. With the fast and furious pace at which information can be thrown at you during a lecture, not to mention the amount of information, it is important that you develop a strategy for recording your notes in an easy-to-follow manner so that you can interpret them later on. The particular style will also depend on the particular class, especially the type of information you're dealing with, how the information is coming at you, and the style of the professor's lecture or textbook author's writing.

The following are some basic format elements that can help you create effective notes. Put an X next to those that you already employ, and a Y next to those that appeal to you and you would like to try.

_____ **Topic headings and subheadings.** The professor typically writes these on the board or states them in phrases like "And now we're going to talk about note taking."

_____ **Examples.** Some are from the book, some are basic, some are exceptions to the rule, some are personal stories from the professor. Note them all so that you have a broad perspective of the concept.

_____ **Connections.** Between topics. Between people. Between events. Between concepts. Between examples. Between theories. Between anything the professor says is connected. Make note of these—even if the connected things have your notes about them on different pages. Arrows and diagrams work great too.

_____ **Tables, charts, graphs, diagrams, time lines, and labeled figures.** If you don't get them on a handout and they're not in the book—draw them in your notes! If the professor draws it, you should draw it. And it makes your notes more interesting.

_____ **Names and dates.** Good to use as headings or subheadings. Make sure you indicate everything else connected to them.

_____ **Formulas, equations, step-by-step problem solving.** Pay close attention to accuracy. If your notes are wrong, you won't have the tools to work your homework problems or complete your lab report.

_____ **Boxes and bubbles.** These are useful when your professor skips around and you need to add additional information to a section of notes you've already completed. Offset the new material neatly by drawing a box or bubble around it so that it's in the original information, but doesn't require that you scribble tiny additions to your neatly organized page.

_____ **Other visual cues.** As your professor emphasizes different points (people, places, events, theories, examples), draw additional attention to them by any means that will make it clearer to you. Underline, circle, draw arrows, smiley faces, stars, exclamation points, etc. Make your notes vivid and eye-catching in relation to the material you'll need to learn.

Cornell: The Most Popular Note-Taking Method

If you aren't familiar with the Cornell Note-Taking Method, you might find it very useful. It is based on the way in which you format your page of notes—where you actually write the information. The purpose is that it will prompt better studying later.

To use this method, you leave a two-and-a-half-inch margin on the left-hand side of your paper. Do not write any information from your text or lecture in this margin. Instead, you will write cues, prompts, or questions related to the notes you took—the answers being clearly discernible by what you have written in the body of your notes. When you fold the page of notes along this margin line or cover it up with another piece of paper, you can create an instant study guide: prompts and questions on one side and the answers hidden by the fold. You can then easily quiz yourself and see how much you know.

Leave a four-inch margin at the bottom of each page. This is for your page summary. After class or completion of a reading assignment, review each page and summarize it briefly in the bottom margin of your page. Use this later for quick reference or to prompt your thinking of the more detailed material.

Naked Exercise #64
Know What to Take Note Of

Students often have the most difficulty in two areas of note taking:

1. Knowing what to write down

2. Getting enough (or too much) information down

Problems with #1 often lead to problems with #2. Here's why.

Many students don't know what's important to write down, so they try to write down *everything* a professor says. Or they may think that everything is important, thus everything should make it onto the paper. This is basically impossible as your transcription skills lag far behind the speed at which your professors can talk. And they never intend for you to write down every word they say. You're not a court reporter. Taking efficient notes takes preparation and *thinking* in order to record all the information you need at a realistic pace.

If you're lucky, your professor will directly tell you what is important to record in your notes. Some will provide an outline on the board or on slides or handouts. Some will write key headings, definitions, names, dates, and theories on the board to make it obvious what you need to know. Good lecturers are very clear, making statements like "Let me give you an example of that" or "An important thing to remember about this theory is..." Capitalize on those moments! Also note when your professors get visibly excited about something—in a good way, or perhaps in an angry rant over a topic. These are clues that show the importance of the issue to your professor, and you are likely to have to know the details.

If you struggle to take good notes, examine how your professor is communicating information to pick clues as to the important information.

Copy this list of items to take with you to each class, then notice each as it occurs.

_____ Handouts are provided with outlines, key names, dates, events, theories, etc.

_____ The professor writes an outline on the board before or during lecture.

_____ The professor writes definitions on the board throughout lecture.

_____ The professor uses explicit language to identify what is important information ("This is important," "You will need to know this," "Write this down," "Let me show you," "Here's an example," "There are three kinds of...," etc.).

_____ The professor uses body language (strong gestures, movement, pointing) to make a point.

_____ The professor underlines, draws arrows, circles, and puts stars next to what he writes on the board for emphasis.

_____ The professor uses phrases like "I think," "In my opinion," "My research found," "I believe," etc.

_____ Your professor references the book by either specific page numbers or more generally ("It states in your book," "The author writes...," etc.).

_____ Your professor references past material ("Last time we were talking about…") to introduce new information.

_____ Your professor uses descriptors like "fascinating," "interesting," "horrifying," "ridiculous," "unbelievable," "incredible," etc., when describing concepts related to the material.

_____ Your professor specifies chronology with phrases like "Step one, step two…," "First, then…," "Start with…," etc.

If you discovered that your professor does a lot of these things, you're on your way. These are great cues for guiding your note taking. These verbal "tags" are indicators that something important is coming and you need to be prepared to write about it. But you don't have to write every word. This is where the thinking comes in. While you listen to what your professor is saying, translate it in your own words and phrases. Writing in ways that make sense to you doesn't require jotting down someone else's every word. In fact, you can develop your own shortcuts if you haven't already. Abbreviations and symbols can make up your own style of shorthand (there 4, u know what u r talking about, even if no 1 else does).

NOTE ABOUT NOTE TAKING: If you are having a hard time taking notes, share your notes with your professor during office hours. Perhaps your professor will give you some tips, or do a better job communicating what's important in class.

Reading Materials = Taking Better Notes

Remember when I mentioned that reading the related assignments either before or soon after class would be helpful? Here's a perfect example. If you have a more complete understanding of the material from your readings, you won't feel the need to write down everything stated in the lecture. Your experience with the text will show you that the information is captured someplace else and at your disposal for studying and review. This will help you be more selective during class as to what you put in your notes.

This goes for taking notes on the readings as well. In many cases your class notes will support the reading material and all you'll have to do is supplement them with some additional examples or connections presented in the book. The point is, the lecture and readings back each other up in terms of giving you the information you need. Take advantage of the multiple sources to lessen the pure _numerical_ demand of note taking (i.e., don't write more words than you have to!). But you must make sure you capture the important content of the material.

Going to Class = Taking Better Notes

You can't take notes if you're not in class. You can always use someone else's, but it's not the same as being there and engaged in the classroom experience. The only way to know your professor's personal preferences when it comes to materials of importance is to go to class. What they think is important, they will emphasize.

THE NOTE-TAKING DANCE PARTY
IS NOW OVER.

**Please shower up and read again when
looking for a good time!**

Designated Doodle Space

Suggested doodle: Draw the dancers above in the box below.

Rate using a scale of 1–10.

> **1 = Not true → 5 = Somewhat true → 10 = Doesn't get any truer**

_____ I know how to read (this is helpful).

_____ I read my daily class reading assignments—daily.

_____ I never get anything out of reading textbooks: they're soooo boring!

_____ I prefer reading the textbook to going to class.

_____ I often have trouble understanding the information in my textbooks.

_____ I enjoy textbooks with lots of charts and graphs and illustrations.

_____ I just can't seem to focus on or "get into" reading books for class.

_____ I can only read when I'm listening to music or there's some kind of background noise.

_____ I have so much reading to do; all I have time for is quickly skimming through the pages.

_____ I read for hours at a time, but don't remember anything.

_____ I love when the material in the book mirrors the information in lecture.

_____ I fall asleep every time I start to read for class.

_____ I like to start at the back of the chapter and read the summary points first.

_____ I just look for all the words in **bold** and read the sentences they're in. That covers all the important stuff.

_____ I can't read without highlighting.

_____ I won't even start to read if I don't have at least an hour to do so.

Naked Exercise #65

What's Your Reading Load (or Overload)?

Welcome to the exercise after the dance party.

I figured you would be tired at this point and might enjoy settling down with a good book (or a not-so-good book that you're required to read).

Do me a favor and get all your course syllabi and look up your current reading assignments. Write down EVERYTHING you are supposed to read—for all your classes—before the next quiz or test. Oh yes...that would be everything you haven't already read and mastered.

Class: _____

Date of next quiz/test: _____

Required reading remaining:

_____

_____

_____

Total number of pages: _____ Number of days to complete: _____

* * *

Class: _____

Date of next quiz/test: _____

Required reading remaining:

_____

_____

_____

Total number of pages: _____ Number of days to complete: _____

* * *

Class: _____

Date of next quiz/test: _____

Required reading remaining:

_____

_____

_____

Total number of pages: _____ Number of days to complete: _____

* * *

Class: _____

Date of next quiz/test: _____

Required reading remaining:

_____

_____

_____

Total number of pages: _____ Number of days to complete: _____

* * *

Class: _____

Date of next quiz/test: _____

Required reading remaining:

_____

_____

_____

Total number of pages: _____ Number of days to complete: _____

Total pages for all classes: _____

Number of days to complete: _____

    If you are like most students, you've got a big number on top and a small number on the bottom. Lots of reading with little time. Welcome to college.

    The primary reason that students end up in this situation is that they put off reading until the last minute—often until it's just too late for it to matter. And why do students put off reading? C'mon, you know...

Naked Exercise #66

Why I Don't Like to Read for Class

I can probably guess why you don't like to do your readings, but I want you to tell me (or rather, yourself).

I don't like to read for class because:

_____

_____

_____

_____

_____

_____

There, feel better? No? Oh...

Now you can see what it is that you have to overcome. Now you can take control of your reading (or rather the *stress* you feel because you aren't reading).

I'm pretty familiar with the reason why most students don't like to read, so I'll address several of them here. Hopefully they'll match your list and it will be like I'm writing this just for you.

Naked Exercise #67

When, Where, and How to Read

Reason #1

I don't like to read for class because I just want to be doing something else.

Reading is just not always the most fun thing to do. Doing it well really requires that you create an environment that helps you do your best reading. Just like the note-taking dance party, do your reading in a place that will make you happy, but will still allow you to concentrate. Some people do their best work alone in a quiet room. Other people like white noise. Some people prefer sitting outside and reading in the main quad or in a quiet place that only they know about.

First, let's take a look at the logistics of your reading. Check which answers apply:

	Habit	Good Idea	Not a Good Idea
_____	I read on my bed.	_____	_____
_____	I read outside.	_____	_____

Habit	Good Idea	Not a Good Idea
_____ I go to the library to read.	_____	_____
_____ I read in my res hall common room.	_____	_____
_____ I am usually alone when I read.	_____	_____
_____ I am usually surrounded by lots of people in the general vicinity of where I read.	_____	_____
_____ I am usually around a small group of people who are doing any number of things while I am trying to read.	_____	_____
_____ I read in absolute silence.	_____	_____
_____ I read with low-level background noise.	_____	_____
_____ I read with music playing.	_____	_____
_____ I read with the television on.	_____	_____
_____ I always get very comfortable when I read.	_____	_____
_____ I make sure I sit at a desk or a table when I read.	_____	_____
_____ I read before I go to bed.	_____	_____
_____ I read between classes.	_____	_____
_____ I read when I eat.	_____	_____
_____ I read while I'm doing something else (cooking, IMing, ironing my clothes).	_____	_____

If you have developed some bad habits in terms of where you read, when you read, and the conditions under which you read, it's time to try something new. With all the reading you are going to have in college, you really need to optimize your fundamental approach to the practice of reading.

Naked Exercise #68

Recalling My Reading Limits

Reason #2

I don't like reading for class because there's just too much of it.

If just looking at your required reading list stresses you out, you aren't alone. Thinking about how long it is likely to take to get through all those pages (and words!) is daunting, and no one gets excited about starting a daunting task. And sometimes our twisted reasoning brings us to the conclusion that if we can't ever finish it, why should we even start it?

If it's time you are concerned about, then you need to go back (sorry) and *read* the section on time management. You need to schedule specific times to read. That may seem too simple a concept, but here's the tricky part: you need to schedule times that don't exceed your optimal reading time. Remember the **Naked Exercise—Knowing Your Limits**? That's the one in which you identified how long you could read for each class without losing focus and daydreaming.

This is absolutely *critical* for planning to read. Only plan to read as long as you are actually going to read productively. If that is only twenty-three minutes, then only schedule reading for twenty-three minutes at a time and do your very best reading!

You can start fresh or go back to the earlier exercise and write your original answer here. For each class, write the length of time you can spend with your textbook and really read to get something out of it. This may vary by class, depending on your interest level in the subject matter and the book itself. Oh, and after you've determined your optimal time, subtract about five to ten minutes to be truly accurate.

Class: _____

I can read with focus and concentrated effort for: _____.

Class: _____

I can read with focus and concentrated effort for: _____.

Class: _____

I can read with focus and concentrated effort for: _____.

Class: _____

I can read with focus and concentrated effort for: _____.

Class: _____

I can read with focus and concentrated effort for: _____.

So the lesson here is to deliberately schedule time to read, but ONLY for periods of time that enable you to be productive—and no longer. Get lots of them on your calendar, but break them up with other activities.

Naked Exercise #69

Helpful Highlighting

Reason #3

I don't like reading for class because it's boring and puts me to sleep.

I can't tell you how to make topics you find uninteresting interesting (dance parties might help), but I can give you some suggestions as to how not to fall asleep when you read.

Most people view reading as a *passive* activity: it involves getting comfortable and sitting still—two ingredients in the recipe for a good nap. So—don't read that way! Get active with the material...work it and learn it. How? Read on.

Maybe you already highlight and still fall asleep, only to wake up with errant yellow markings on your arms, clothes, and possibly the margins of your book (yellow markings on clothes under the desks mean you MUST do laundry!). If you are falling asleep, you are doing it wrong.

Highlighting is intended to make you think before you mark. Again, highlighting is intended to make you think before you mark. Interesting (that's why I said it twice).

You have to consider what you have just read, relative to everything else you've just read, and determine if it carries enough weight to highlight for future reference. You can't do that well when you're only half conscious.

The reason that most students don't highlight correctly—or perhaps I should say *effectively*—is because they mark their books up indiscriminately. They just put the pen to paper and drag. When you do this almost every line in every paragraph, you are simply in a rote mechanical mode and the repetition numbs your senses.

Of course, you're not actually thinking about anything either. If everything seems equally as important, you are not gaining what you need to from your time.

It's time to see what you've learned about highlighting, so go get your favorite (or your only) highlighter and come back here. If you don't have a highlighter, go back to the bookstore and get yourself one. You can use this box below to sample the highlighters.

Remember, highlighting should prompt you to be active with your reading, so you don't have to limit yourself to just one color. To really keep on your toes, stay awake, and learn the information as you read it, consider using a variety of colored highlighters to emphasize different elements of the material. For example, you can use blue to highlight all names of important people, green to highlight all significant dates, pink to highlight theories, yellow to highlight events, and orange to highlight related research studies.

Are you imagining a lot of grabbing, uncapping, writing, re-capping, reading, grabbing another pen, then starting the process all over again? If so—very good— that's the idea! This should be a very active, engaging process, one in which you must think about what you are reading, consider what should be highlighted, then categorize the important points as you go along.

Now go back through this highlighting section (only the material under the heading "Helpful Highlighting") and highlight just the key points. It's not a lot of information, but you really need to think about the ideas and concepts that stand out. At the end of this section on reading, I'll share what you should have highlighted. But do it on your own, right now.

PLEASE DO YOUR HIGHLIGHTING NOW.

Reason #4

I don't like reading for class because I have a hard time understanding the material.

First be aware that it's just a fact that some textbooks are better written than others. Not everyone who is knowledgeable in a field of study (and is asked to write a book) is a savvy writer. And it stinks to get one of their books (I hope this book is not one of them). I mention that so you don't feel too bad if you struggle with a book; it truly may be the author's fault (again, don't blame me or Harlan for your lack of interest in this one. I mean, we turned note taking into a dance party...).

Unfortunately, not understating the material doesn't free you from having to read and learn the material in the book. So how can you adapt to a challenging book with difficult material? Several ways.

Grab a few of your textbooks to work with for the next few exercises, perhaps the ones that you find most difficult. Open a book to any chapter. What do you see? Flip through the pages. Turn to the end of the chapter. Do you notice anything...interesting? What stands out? Is there more to each page than lines of uninterrupted text? Is there anything that draws your attention away from the paragraph-heavy content of each section?

Typically textbook chapters have lots of additional "features"—elements that kick off the chapter, blurbs in the margins, and a collection of bits and pieces of material tagged on at the end of all that seemingly endless dry academic prose.

Look through each of your books and identify which of the following features they contain. Look both at the beginning of the chapter, throughout the contents pages, and at the end of each chapter.

Chapter Feature	Textbook #1	Textbook #2	Textbook #3	Textbook #4
Chapter outline	_____	_____	_____	_____
List of things "you will learn"	_____	_____	_____	_____
Chapter objectives	_____	_____	_____	_____

Chapter Feature	Textbook #1	Textbook #2	Textbook #3	Textbook #4
List of key terms	_____	_____	_____	_____
Cognitive (visual) map of concepts	_____	_____	_____	_____
Stories or vignettes	_____	_____	_____	_____
Personal profile	_____	_____	_____	_____
Online exercises/resources	_____	_____	_____	_____
Charts, graphs, tables, illustrations	_____	_____	_____	_____
Brief section/chapter summary	_____	_____	_____	_____
Term definitions	_____	_____	_____	_____
Key person index	_____	_____	_____	_____
Review questions	_____	_____	_____	_____
Other	_____	_____	_____	_____

Did you discover anything interesting in your exploration? Have you ever paid attention to these features? If you are like most students, you will have ignored all of these extras, and when it's time to read, you just dive in to the main bulk of the content. But these features are there for a reason, and that is to help you understand the material better as you read it. They also work to keep you active as you read and, therefore, spending your time productively. Here's how it works.

Whatever particular features your textbook presents, they are there to provide you a *context* with which to better understand the information. Our brains need a context or a framework in which we can place new information so that it makes sense. When you just plow headfirst into the material without even looking at the title of the chapter, you won't get the full point of what the words are trying to convey. You may understand all the words, know the vocabulary, and get the grammatical structure of the sentences, but if you don't realize that "Make sure you take it off before there's a huge mess" is referring to a boiling pot of potatoes on the stove rather than a white shirt before eating a bowl of spaghetti, you will essentially be lost. Imagine this scenario when reading about psychoanalysis, Bernoulli's principle, or the Kreb's Cycle.

When you take the time to read the chapter outline or familiarize yourself with the chapter objectives, *you prepare yourself for what you're about to read.* When your brain knows what's coming—the subject matter, the elements of that subject, and how those elements are related—it will call up everything it already knows about that subject. When you go into reading with what you already know, everything that follows will make more sense. You have your *framework* within which to place the information you encounter on the page.

The other features—key terms, definitions, people's names, brief summaries—all contribute to your understanding of the chapter material in the same way. But they won't work if you don't read them FIRST.

Naked Exercise #71

Taking Advantage of the Features

This Naked Exercise is about getting to know your textbooks' best features. Take a few minutes to read through any features presented at the beginning of the chapter (an outline, objectives list, etc.). Then read several pages into the chapter. Really pay attention to how what you read in the feature helped you gain more from the main text.

Write a brief summary about what you discovered after using the features in your text.

Features used prior to reading:

_____

_____

_____

What I noticed about my reading that followed:

_____

_____

_____

When you selected your features, did you just stick to those at the beginning of the chapter? Did you explore those at the end of the chapter? Sometimes it can be even more helpful to read through the elements at the *end* of the chapter before you start at the beginning. This is because the end will tell you (or quiz you on) the important information that you should have gained from the previous reading. Then you can keep an eye out for it. But if you haven't read it yet, then you won't know what you should be looking for when you do read.

And this is one of the biggest keys to turning *passive* reading into *active* reading. Reading with the purpose of learning specific things, or finding answers to particular questions, gives you a task to do while you read.

Naked Exercise #72

Read and Review

Find a chapter in one of your books that has a set of review questions at the end of it. Write the review questions down here, then start reading at the beginning of the chapter until you find all the answers (which you will also write down here).

Review question #1:

_____

Answer (found on page):

_____

_____

_____

Review question #2:

_____

Answer (found on page):

_____

_____

_____

Review question #3:

_____

Answer (found on page):

_____

_____

_____

Review question #4:

_____

Answer (found on page):

_____

_____

_____

How did you do? Did you find it easier to read given that you had a specific goal in mind? Did it make the material easier to understand since you had a context to place it in and a particular aspect of the information to seek out? If you felt a greater sense of purpose with your reading and you felt more engaged with the information, consider starting all of your reading at the end of the chapter—with the review questions.

Naked Exercise #73

Use Those Headings and Subheadings

As you browse through your chapters, you can identify the different section headings and subheadings. Don't ignore these in your haste to move on to the next section (so that you can hurry up and finish your reading). You can actually *use* these headings to help you get more out of your reading. Not only are they critical to providing that mental context I told you about, but they can also be a tool for you to read more actively.

Select a chapter that you haven't read yet. For every heading and subheading, rewrite it as a question. I'll start you off with an example.

Heading/Subheading: "Use Those Headings and Subheadings"

Question: Why are headings and subheadings important?

For a more academic example:

Heading/Subheading: "The Parts of a Cell"

Question: What are the parts of a cell?

Your Turn

Heading/Subheading: _____

Question: _____

Heading/Subheading: _____

Question: _____

Heading/Subheading: _____

Question: _____

Heading/Subheading: _____

Question: _____

Heading/Subheading: _____

Question: _____

So can you guess the next step? Once you create your questions, you simply read the text that follows the heading or subheading with the goal of answering your question. In creating the questions (clearly an easy task) you will more directly gain what is intended from each particular section. You read in order to find the answer—and you will.

If you use the features at your disposal, you will change the way you *work with the reading material*. And that is very different from simply sitting and reading.

One More Subheading about Reading

There are some features I didn't talk about—such as online exercises, charts, graphs, vignettes—which all offer options to help you work actively with your text. Find the features that appeal to you most and start by reading or looking through them. Branch out from the information presented there to reading the related material. It will be more meaningful and interesting.

Rate using a scale of 1–10.

_____ I never have enough time to study.

_____ I have no specific strategies for studying; I just "wing it."

_____ I dread sitting down to review my notes before a test—I usually fall asleep.

_____ I save all of my studying until the day or two before the exam—that's the only way I'll remember it.

_____ I find studying with others helpful.

_____ I can't concentrate for very long periods of time.

_____ I usually don't end up reading all my assigned reading before an exam.

_____ I use specific tools to help me prepare for my exams.

_____ I begin studying many days before an exam and feel well prepared by test time.

_____ I study by doing lots of memorizing.

_____ I believe that effective studying requires long periods of intense, focused concentration.

_____ I have a hard time trying to figure out what I should study for in order to prepare for an exam.

_____ I don't know how to "study" from my notes or the readings. I just try to read and memorize as much of the information as I can.

_____ I don't do well in study groups because they always turn into social events.

_____ I would never ask my professor how to study for the test.

_____ I don't need help studying.

Naked Exercise #74

How You Study, Plain and Simple

That's right, there are *strategies* for studying. This means you will need to study the strategies to study. Taking the time to study studying will help you learn material more effectively, manage your time better, and reduce your stress (really!).

Most students have a routine approach they take when it's time (or past the time) to study for an exam. Somehow you've gotten to college. You must have a routine. List all the things you generally do, in the order you do them, when preparing for an exam.

My Study Techniques	Number of Days Prior to Exam
_____	_____
_____	_____
_____	_____
_____	_____
_____	_____

The next question is—do these techniques work?

Maybe you do them out of habit, maybe you do them because you don't really know what else to do, or maybe you do them because they really are effective for you. Just so that you can really own this, go back and circle those techniques that are truly helpful for mastering exam material, and place an X next to the techniques that honestly aren't worthwhile.

Now that you've connected with your current approach to studying, it will put you in the frame of mind to learn more about different strategies for studying. Are you ready? I can't hear you. Are you ready?! I still can't hear you. (Of course, this is a book so I'll never be able to hear you.)

Naked Exercise #75

A Test for You (That's Right, a Test)

This is a closed-book, closed-notes, closed-laptop test. No cheating, just use what you know to complete the following:

1. In the space below, write the words to the "Star-Spangled Banner." (You may have to write small.)

_____

_____

_____

_____

_____

2. In the space below, write the lyrics to your favorite song (assuming your favorite song is NOT also the "Star-Spangled Banner").

_____

_____

_____

_____

_____

OK, that's enough. Now check your answers (feel free to use the Internet now). My guess is that you don't need to; you got them both correct (or at least the one with the lyrics to your favorite song). So, when did you study for this test? You couldn't have known it was coming, so how was it that you did so well?

Of course, you already knew the answers. But how did you come to know them? At what point did you spend time studying the lyrics to either our national anthem or your favorite song? If your answer is "never," think about how cool that is! You learned something significant and important, without ever having to study! Wouldn't you like to do that with everything you have to learn? Well, you can. And it won't even require music. (Although that's always a nice bonus if you can sing what you know.)

Naked Exercise #76

Learn to Study and Have It Not Feel Like Studying

How do you think you learned all those lyrics without making much of an effort? Might it have been the fact that when you discovered your new favorite song, you immediately downloaded it to your iPod and listened to it over and over again? You probably weren't ever trying to learn the words—or at least you didn't set out to work hard at it, but it happened simply through your constant exposure to them. You can apply the same principle to learning material from class. All it requires is a little time and your willingness to do it.

Here's what you do.

From the first day of each new unit you begin in class (a unit being the set of material that the next test will cover), you will simply read through the notes you have taken so far. To do this, you will only need a few minutes at the beginning, and probably no more than fifteen to twenty right before test time. Begin by finding one of your swiss cheese time "holes" (or hole-in-the-sock times) to work this in every day. Suggestions are:

- While you are eating
- While you are waiting for your next class to start
- While you are waiting for your friend to meet you somewhere
- While you are on the treadmill
- While you are brushing your teeth (don't drip toothpaste on your notes, though)
- While you are standing in line at the bank.

How It Works

The first day you are only likely to have three to five pages of notes. All you do is read through them. Do not try to memorize anything. Do not study each word intensely for several minutes. Just casually, but fully, read them. For three to five pages this will only take you a few minutes.

The next day following class, you will do the same thing, making sure to start on the first page of notes. Yes, that's right—the ones you read on the first day. You read through the first day's notes, then on to the notes from the second day of lecture. Now it will take you a little longer, but not much.

The third day of lecture (and you can certainly do this on non-lecture days too!) you will do it again—starting on Day 1 and casually reading everything through the latest lecture notes you have. Remember, this shouldn't stress you out, cause you mental fatigue, or any kind of intellectual duress whatsoever. You are just reading. But soon you will discover something. You will be *bored* with the notes from Day 1. After awhile you will be completely tired of reading notes from the second lecture. And so on. Why is this? BECAUSE YOU KNOW IT! And you came to know it without much time or effort at all!

Imagine that you are into the third week of the unit and your test is a week away. Students always forget what was talked about in the early days of a new set of material and have a hard time recalling it when it's time to study for the exam. But not you! You will open your notebook to page one, and at this point, you are likely to be able to recite every term and definition, know every important person and what he or she did, rattle off significant dates, events, and theories, and list the unfolding order of various processes. In fact, you may HATE starting on the first page of notes every time you sit down to read through them, because you are so tired of the material. But that's a very good thing.

This will enable you to accomplish several important things:

- Keep up with the material so that you are ready for the subsequent material presented in class each day, and understand it better in context.
- Develop a sense of control and reduce your stress level. Each time you read through your notes, you will feel like you have accomplished something. You'll know you've taken a small step to being ready for the exam.
- Establish a source of motivation to prompt you to do more. When you keep up with the information and feel that you are on top of what you need to know, you will want to continue doing what works.
- Provide the foundation for learning the information that is presented later in the unit. Having the time to "get bored" with the early concepts, the fact that you will have less time to reach that level with the later material won't be a problem. Your thorough knowledge and comfort level with the older concepts will help you make meaning out of the new information and remember it in that way. Plus, you are introduced to that material much closer to test time.

Naked Exercise #77

How to Learn without Really Trying

Get your binder from one of your classes in which you take a lot of notes. Open to the first page of your newest unit (the start of notes for information covered on the next exam). Look at your watch—if you have a stopwatch function, even better—and note the time. Casually begin reading through your notes, pay attention to the information, but don't attempt to memorize anything. When you've reached the end of one lecture's worth of material, see how long it took you.

Next, quiz yourself by thinking through everything you can remember (new terms, people's names, dates, steps in a process, etc.) Feel free to jot it down if you want. You'll probably be pleasantly surprised.

Continue to do this each day for the next week—always starting your reading on the first page of your notes and continuing through the last page of notes you've taken to that point, timing yourself as you go. Self-test each day to see how much you remember, and you are likely to find that you know a great deal, particularly about the information presented early on in the unit.

Day	Start Time	End Time	Total	Amount I Retained		
1	_____	_____	_____	Little	Moderate	Significant
2	_____	_____	_____	Little	Moderate	Significant
3	_____	_____	_____	Little	Moderate	Significant
4	_____	_____	_____	Little	Moderate	Significant
5	_____	_____	_____	Little	Moderate	Significant
6	_____	_____	_____	Little	Moderate	Significant
7	_____	_____	_____	Little	Moderate	Significant

How did this work for you? What did you discover about using this simple (and time efficient) method of learning without really trying?

_____

_____

_____

So, to really make this work, you have to do the following:

1. Keep your class notes with you at all times.

2. Commit to finding pockets of time every day or every other day to read your notes.

3. Start from your first page of notes every time, no matter how tired of them you are.

4. Stick with it.

Naked Exercise #78

Define "Active Studying"

Most students will say they tend to fall asleep when studying. Unless you're participating in a sleep study, this won't help you pass class (and no, sleeping on a textbook doesn't allow for material to be absorbed). You need to turn the word *study* from a passive verb to an active verb. It shouldn't put you to sleep.

Write your definition and provide specific examples of what you believe "active studying" is.

Active studying is:

_____

_____

_____

Some examples of active study techniques are:

_____

_____

_____

Hopefully, you'll find your examples in the upcoming section (which means you have discovered some productive ways to learn material), but if you struggled with this one, here are some ideas.

Active study means that you *work* with the information that you have to learn. It's like working in this workbook. It's the purpose of the workbook. You can read anything, and for a brief nanosecond, a concept can touch your conscious mind. But, if you simply continue reading passively, you'll lose sight of the concepts and not remember them. Do something while you read to help you engage with the reading.

When you *do* something with a concept you read, then it gives you the opportunity to learn that concept. Being active with it keeps it bouncing around in your brain long enough to make it into your memory. Instead of logging on to Facebook when you need a break in your studying, you can draw a picture of what you just read. Make it *meaningful* to you and it will be easier to remember.

So how do you get *active* with class material? Any way that you'd like! But here are some ideas to get you started.

Highlighting

We covered this earlier, but highlighting is active. Especially if you come up with a color-code system. You might use blue for concepts, yellow for dates, orange for people, pink for processes, green for theories, etc. As you read your class notes and textbook, have your pens on the ready to color away. And keep this in mind: It is less about the colored highlighting and more about the *exposure* to the material and the fact that you are looking for specific things as you read. And an added bonus, there might just be a special guy or girl who sees you with your all your highlighters and wants to join in on the highlighter action.

Flash Cards

Flash cards may seem like something best used to help third graders learn their multiplication tables, but they are actually a great way to actively work with course material that you need to learn.

Again, the process of *making* the flash cards in and of itself is a great way to expose yourself to the information with little effort (like reading your class notes daily). In fact, it is probably something you can productively do while listening to music, sitting around with friends, or watching your favorite television show.

Keep a set of index cards with you at all times, so that you can be ready to add to your collection at any time, anywhere (like while eating a bagel on a bench between classes). You can also make use of your colored highlighting to easily see the categories for your cards. Once you've made the cards, keep them with you so that you can flip through them quickly and easily. The more you see the information, the sooner you'll learn it, and with little effort.

Tables, Charts, and Graphs—Oh My!

Reading information written out in sentences and long paragraphs can be uninspiring and put you to sleep. But when you can see it laid out in a table, formatted in a chart, or presented in a graph, it is likely to engage your attention much more actively. This is because you have to assess what the format itself is conveying, and interpret the information from that particular perspective. For many students, this makes working with the material much more interesting.

But if your professor or the textbook doesn't present the material in any of these graphic ways, you can create them for yourself. This is yet another active exercise to get you working with the material so that you can gain more exposure to it while you do the task, and it provides a useful tool to study from later on.

Naked Exercise #79

Get Graphic with Your Information

Grab some paper, your textbook, or class notes from a course in which you have an exam in the near future. Look for ways to present the information in some kind of graphic format. There are no rules for this, just determine the ways that it makes sense to you and see what you can create.

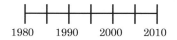

Try to find information that you can present in each of the following ways:

- Time line
- Pie chart
- Table
- Graph
- Venn diagram
- Cognitive map
- Figure

If you are a visual learner, you will really enjoy this kind of active studying. Also, if you are artistic, you should like to work with information in this way. And again, one of the key benefits to doing these *activities* is that they can be done without heavy, intense mental concentration, they are enjoyable enough for you to want to engage in them, and they give you more exposure to the material.

Your Turn

Pick a new active way to study.

1. What method did you pick?

_____

_____

_____

2. How did this help you?

_____

_____

_____

3. What surprised you about this?

_____

_____

_____

Naked Exercise #80

Find Your Study Buddies

Studying with classmates can either be VERY effective or a big waste of time. There are some study groups that are more about pretending to study than actually getting work done—these are groups where people sit around books pretending to get things done. These groups can get you a boyfriend or girlfriend, but not always the grade you desire.

The key to a successful study group is the people in it. You gain from study groups only if the members of the group have something to contribute. Pick your group members carefully and deliberately. This means, identify the people in your class who will bring something valuable to the group. These are:

- the students who are always in class and on time
- the students who ask a lot of insightful questions in class
- the students who answer a lot of questions in class
- the students who sit near the front
- the students who chat with the professor before and/or after class

If you are not someone in class asking questions, answering questions, sitting near the front of the class, and chatting with the professor, it's possible no one will want *you* in their study group! So it's important to both *be* this kind of student and to *get to know* this kind of student. If you don't already know these types of people in class, take action now to sit next to one in class and introduce yourself. Once you've identified a few strong students, invite them for a study session. You can be the one to start the group.

Think of your study groups like an athletic team (without the profuse sweating and matching shirts and shorts). Consider who you would like to study with before the next test. Even if you don't know their names, write a physical description (the cute girl with the red hair, tattoo of Lady Gaga on her neck, and the Hello Kitty backpack). The goal is to see if you've identified some potentially valuable study mates in each class.

Class: _____   Class: _____

Students I would like to study with: Students I would like to study with:

_____   _____

_____   _____

_____   _____

_____   _____

* * *

Class: _____   Class: _____

Students I would like to study with: Students I would like to study with:

_____   _____

_____   _____

_____   _____

_____   _____

* * *

Class: _____   Class: _____

Students I would like to study with: Students I would like to study with:

_____   _____

_____   _____

_____   _____

_____   _____

Naked Exercise #81

Creating a Study Group Preparedness Plan

Now that you've identified your study dream-team, get to know them before the next test and plan a time to get together. And then when you meet as a group, be prepared to put together a Study Group Preparedness Plan.

This is important, because even the most motivated students can lose focus in a group. Socializing takes over and the focus shifts to Facebook and YouTube videos unrelated to class. Yes, a little socializing is normal, but there needs to be a focus.

One major reason that study groups often fall apart is because students don't go into the groups with a specific *plan*. Everyone just gets together and brings their notebooks and a textbook or two and...then what? If you can't answer this question, you're likely not to get much learning out of it. So how do you make a plan?

You simply consider what you want to accomplish. As a group, discuss—and identify—the following:

1. How long will the study session last? _____

   _____

   _____

2. Where will the study session take place? _____

   _____

3. What is each person's primary goal for the study session (i.e., what does each person want to leave having accomplished or having learned)?

   Member A: _____

   Member B: _____

   Member C: _____

   Member D: _____

4. How will the session be structured? What will group members do?

First we will: _____

Second we will: _____

Third we will: _____

Fourth we will: _____

5. What will each member's role be in order to accomplish the goals of the group?

Facilitator (mediates discussion, provides prompts for input, etc.):

_____

Time keeper (keeps track of time to accomplish goals, alerts group to wrap up, move on to the next topic, etc.):

_____

Materials manager (looks through notes and texts to identify relevant information, reads passages as necessary, organizes group members' sources of information, etc.):

_____

Reporter (identifies common questions, summarizes conclusions, restates ideas for clarification, etc.):

_____

It's not always necessary to be this structured, but when you take a more deliberate approach to what you want to accomplish as a group and how you will accomplish it, you will find the group is much more productive and time invested is worthwhile.

Don't rely entirely on study groups for your test preparation, but consider adding them to your arsenal of active study strategies. When done right they can be productive and enjoyable, and connect you with great students in your classes.

Naked Exercise #82

Welcome to Dr. [Your Name Here]'s Class

You may have heard that one of the best ways to learn anything is by teaching it to others. One of the best ways to study (learn) is to pretend to lecture on the material (teach it) to others (your cat, stuffed teddy bear, or picture of your boyfriend or girlfriend). And when I say "lecture," I mean to say it OUT LOUD. It doesn't have to be that loud (be kind to your neighbors), but it does have to be audible so that you can hear what you are saying.

Even though you don't have a real audience, when you pretend to lecture to others with the goal of teaching them unfamiliar material (like your professor does for you), you will find that you actually anticipate their questions. When you imagine what someone might ask while you are lecturing, you force yourself to be really clear, define what you are talking about, and explicitly state connections between concepts.

When you do this, get up and walk around! BE the professor! Have your notes open on a table or your dresser, glance at them to get the topic, then look away from them to your imagined audience and teach! When you need to refresh your memory about a concept or definition, refer back to your notes. But otherwise, approach "studying" with the goal of teaching the material to others *in your own words*. And if you'd like to make this real, have the person you're talking to text on his phone, browse the Internet, and look completely uninterested. You'll see just what it means to have class in the classroom.

Now it's time for you to try it. If you are working in this workbook on your own, find a quiet space where you can be alone and lecture (out loud) about this section to your heart's content. Just get a feel for it. Keep the workbook handy so you can glance at it for support, but as you refresh what you know, present the information in your own words.

If you are working in this workbook for class, your instructor may give you the opportunity to lecture briefly to your classmates for practice. Be prepared, and imagine all of the ways that you would like your professors to be more engaging speakers—and do it!

It might feel a bit awkward at first, but once you get used to this method of studying, you'll enjoy it and discover just how effective it is.

THE NAKED STUDY SECTION IS OVER!!!!

Hallelujah, Hallelujah, Hallelujah, Hallelujahhhhhhhhh

Rate using a scale of 1–10.

> **1** = Not true → **5** = Somewhat true → **10** = Doesn't get any truer

_____ I have more money than I'll ever need.

_____ I have several unique things about me that might qualify me for a scholarship or special aid.

_____ I know how to balance my budget.

_____ I have no idea what kinds of financial aid are available or if I would be eligible for anything.

_____ I have to work full time to put myself through school.

_____ I have a meal plan for the dining hall, but I don't use it much because I'd rather eat out.

_____ There is a really fun, cool department on campus that I would love to work in.

_____ I am very good at managing my money.

_____ I just spend whatever I've got and ask Mom and Dad for more.

_____ I use my credit card for everything!

_____ I only charge what I know I can pay off when the bill comes.

_____ I don't want the responsibility (or temptation) of a credit card.

_____ Most of my extra money goes for food.

_____ I often don't know where my money goes.

_____ I know what compound interest is.

_____ I always have to have the latest "stuff."

Naked Exercise #83

Loans, Grants, Scholarships, and Loose Change

There's money out there. You just have to go after it.

Money isn't a problem until you run out of it (usually around the second month of school). Student debt is a concern. According to a 2012 report from the Federal Reserve Bank of New York:

> The outstanding student loan balance now stands at about $870 billion, surpassing the total credit card balance ($693 billion) and the total auto loan balance ($730 billion). This balance is expected to continue its upward trend.

Money is one of the more important issues in your life. It's not evil; it's necessary. You need money to pay for college, buy (or rent) your books, and eat. It helps to have money or to know how to get some.

There is money out there, but you have to spend your time working to get it. Scholarships, grants, and loose change help. If you say you don't have time to apply for scholarships and grants, think about it in terms of your time. A few hundred dollars for a couple of hours of paperwork is worth it—right?

What you don't know about financial aid can cost you. Let's start with a quick financial quiz. Knowing the answers can save you lots of money.

1. Who is eligible to receive federal financial aid?

_____

_____

2. What is a federal student loan and what is a private student loan?

_____

_____

3. What is a grant?

_____

_____

4. What is a scholarship?

_____

_____

5. What is the difference between a grant and a loan?

_____

_____

6. What is the difference between a loan and a scholarship?

_____

_____

7. Why is it better to have a scholarship and grant rather than a loan?

_____

_____

8. What are three ways you can lose your financial aid?

_____

_____

Answers to the Financial Quiz (Don't Cheat)

1. To receive federal student aid, you must meet certain requirements. You must:

    - be a U.S. citizen or eligible noncitizen.
    - have a valid social security number (unless you're from the Republic of the Marshall Islands, the Federated States of Micronesia, or the Republic of Palau).
    - be registered with Selective Service if you are male and eighteen to twenty-five years of age (go to www.sss.gov for more information).
    - have a high school diploma or a General Education Development (GED) Certificate or pass an exam approved by the U.S. Department of Education.
    - be enrolled or accepted for enrollment as a regular student working toward a degree or certificate in an eligible program at a school that participates in the federal student aid programs.
    - not have a drug conviction for an offense that occurred while you were receiving federal student aid (such as grants, loans, or work-study).
    - not owe a refund on a federal grant or be in default on a federal student loan.
    - demonstrate financial need (except for unsubsidized Stafford Loans).
    - Other requirements may apply. Contact your school's financial aid office for more information.

2. A student loan is a sum of money to be used for academic expenses. The loan must be paid back with interest. There are Federal Stafford Loans, Federal PLUS loans (no financial need is required), and campus-based programs (work-study, Federal Supplemental Educational Opportunity Grant, and the Federal Perkins Loan). In the case of a subsidized Stafford Loan (demonstrated need for the loan), the student is not responsible for interest while attending at least half-time and the principal is deferred. If it is an unsubsidized Stafford Loan (financial need was not demonstrated), the principal is still deferred but the student is responsible for paying interest on the loan.

3. A grant is a financial award given to students from the government that does not have to be repaid. There are Federal Pell Grants, Academic Competitiveness Grants, National Science & Mathematics Access to Retain Talent Grants, and Teach Education Assistance for College and Higher

Education Grants. There is also the federal work-study program. This allows students enrolled in college to work and receive financial compensation.

4. A scholarship is a financial award. Some scholarships are need-based while others are awarded based on other criteria. There are athletic scholarships, academic scholarships, and thousands of other kinds of scholarships available based on a student's unique accomplishments and traits.

5. Assuming you don't get arrested for drugs, a grant doesn't need to be paid back. A loan must be paid back (oftentimes with interest).

6. A loan needs to be paid back. A scholarship does not need to be paid back.

7. You don't want to have to pay back money.

8. Poor grades, a drug conviction, not participating in the sport for which the scholarship was awarded.

Cha-Ching: The Scholarship

Are you a musician with six fingers and have grandparents who were born in Hungary who worked on the railroad when they came to the United States of America? If so, you qualify for the Six-Finger Hungarian Musical Train scholarship!

Yes, there are literally thousands of scholarships out there that can be within reach (and with six fingers you can hold onto even more scholarships). There are scholarships that are tied to religion, race, ethnicity, interests, academics, and other unique characteristics or talents. Many are not all that publicized, so you have to do some digging to find them.

But because most students don't do the digging for the cash, the money can go unused. For those students who do make the effort and apply for these scholarships, the odds are in their favor to win the scholarship lotto. (And for the record, I made up the six-finger music scholarship.)

Consider ways in which you might be unique enough to qualify for a "hidden" scholarship.

_____ Religion (Christian, Jewish, Muslim, Seventh Day Adventist, Methodist, Catholic, etc.)

_____ Musical talent and accomplishments (choir, band, orchestra—or your specific instrument: bassoon, viola, marimba, castanets)

_____ Sports (some of the lesser-known ones: shot put, field hockey, lacrosse, water polo)

_____ Organization membership (Girl and Boy Scouts, Camp Fire, Toastmasters, 4-H)

_____ Parents' organization membership (Shriners, VFW, Daughters of the American Revolution)

_____ Hobbies (photography, dance, theater...things that are not your college major, but that you've been involved in)

_____ College major

_____ Ethnicity or family heritage (Native American, Polish-American, Hispanic, Nordic—even if you are just a percentage of a certain nationality, you may qualify)

_____ Parents' occupations

_____ City or town residence

_____ High school involvement (Key Club, Latin Club, FBLA, FFA, etc.)

_____ Community service work

_____ Your employer (grocery store, video store, book store—even for just a summer job)

_____ A parent's employer / company scholarship or grant program

Students of all ages can be eligible for scholarships. There are need-based scholarships and there are award-based scholarships. To apply, be ready to write a good essay and highlight your connection to the organization giving the money, your accomplishments so far, and the worthwhile way in which you will use the money.

Scholarship #1:

Name of scholarship: _____

Application requirement(s): _____

_____

Deadline for submission: _____

Campus contact who can review before you submit your application: _____

_____

* * *

Scholarship #2:

Name of scholarship: _____

Application requirement(s): _____

_____

Deadline for submission: _____

Campus contact who can review before you submit your application: _____

_____

* * *

Scholarship #3:

Name of scholarship: _____

Application requirement(s): _____

_____

Deadline for submission: _____

Campus contact who can review before you submit your application: _____

_____

NAKED NOTE TO READERS: The Naked Journal is back in this section. To make life easier, we kept the numbering the same as the Naked Exercise. If you feel deprived because there are no journals in the study section, feel free to create your own and insert them in the previous section. Yeah, that sounds like a fantastic idea...

✎ Naked Journal #83: Not a Bad Day's Work

This journal entry will take a little bit of work.

Step #1: Talk to your friends, teaching assistants, and the people in the financial aid office to locate someone who has received a scholarship. Ask this person how he or she became aware of the scholarship. Have him or her explain the application process in detail. Find out how long it took to complete the process, what kind of work was involved, how long it took to apply for the scholarship, and how long it took to receive an award or a rejection. Find out how much money the recipient was awarded for his or her efforts. Then ask the recipient to guess the total number of hours spent applying for ALL scholarships and the total amount awarded.

Step #2: Now the fun part. Calculate how much this work was rewarded on an hourly basis. For example, someone who received $5,000 for five hours' worth of work can say that he or she earned $1,000 an hour. Not a bad day's work.

Step #3: Write this in the form of a story. The last line of your story (following the hourly wage calculation) is "Not a bad day's work!"

Naked Exercise #84

Your Financial Aid Advisor: Money, Money, Money, Monnneeeey

Your financial aid advisor knows where the money is and how to get you as much of it as possible. Form a close and trusting relationship with your advisor and trust that you will know how to get as much money as possible.

Most people look to their financial advisors only when they are in a financial pickle (that's not a real pickle, it's a baseball expression for being in a jam). But you should make sure you schedule time to get to know your financial advisors before and after you *need* money. Build a relationship, and you will see the rewards.

One thing that will help you have something to talk about with your advisor is having an understanding of what you need or want money for. If you are looking for extra cash to pimp out your room to compete with the guys in the next suite over, you're not likely to be well received. If you barely have enough to pay for classes and books, and need money to help you afford to live on campus, that's a different story.

Given your current financial situation, check all of the following items that you will need money for this year:

_____ Tuition and fees

_____ Books and supplies

_____ Housing

_____ Transportation to and from school

_____ Spending money for gas, groceries, basic entertainment

_____ Dues for a campus organization (fraternity/sorority, club, etc.)

_____ Study abroad

_____ Other _____

_____ Other _____

_____ Other _____

Now that you've identified areas where you need financial assistance, think about your options for obtaining the funds. There may be many possibilities available to you, so consider those that you would be most willing to do in order to get the money you need.

Rank the following in order of your preference:

_____ Getting a loan and paying it back after college

_____ Spending some time doing research to uncover rarely publicized scholarship money

_____ Getting a part-time job on campus to earn the money

_____ Getting a part-time job off campus to earn the money

_____ Asking Mom and Dad or Grandma and Grandpa or Great Aunt Sally for the money

_____ Selling bodily fluids, hair, or organs

_____ I'll do any or all of these!

What Next?

Option 1:
Visit the Financial Aid Office on your campus to determine what loan or grant programs you qualify for. The advisors will provide you with all the information you need regarding how much you can receive and when you will be required to pay it back. Your advisor may have information on some scholarship opportunities, but your independent research is likely to uncover scholarship gold.

Option 2:
Consider taking on a part-time job. Visit the Career Center on campus for options. The Career Center is often the point of contact for finding what jobs are available to students on campus, and opportunities for students in the local community. Career counselors can help you identify jobs that fit your schedule and possibly even relate to your major or areas of interest. They may even connect you with a paid internship opportunity in which you can earn money while getting experience in your field.

If you do decide to find a job, set your sights on a campus job. It's a fact that students who work on campus are more engaged with the campus community and tend to do better in their academics. Depending on where you work, you may have the opportunity to meet and get to know faculty, staff, and other students. Being a part of a particular office, department, or business on campus is a great way to earn your money and connect more with your university. (To learn more, check out the next exercise!)

Option 3:
Talk to other students and upperclassmen. The students who have been there and done it can help you figure out how to do it. In fact, because they did it themselves, they can help you find answers even more efficiently. They can also connect you with the best financial aid advisors and professionals to help you find more money.

Before you meet with either the Financial Aid Office or the Career Center, you'll want to be able to tell your financial story.

Overview of your financial situation:

Sources of income (semester/monthly/weekly):

1. _____

2. _____

3. _____

4. _____

5. _____

Things I need more money for (see items checked):

1. _____

2. _____

3. _____

4. _____

5. _____

Identify the following:

Where is the Financial Aid Office located on your campus?

_____

What is the name and phone number of a financial aid officer (advisor)?

_____

Where is the Career Center located on your campus?

_____

What is the name and phone number of a career counselor?

_____

Take the next step:

Appointment time with financial aid advisor:

✎ Naked Journal #84: Love/Hate Relationship with Money

Everyone has a unique relationship with money. Some people love money and some people hate it (the people with not enough tend to be the ones who hate it). Explain your love or hate relationship with money. What events in your life have helped shape this relationship? How have your parents impacted this relationship? How have your friends' relationship with money impacted you? Share a story that illustrates your loving or not-so-loving relationship with money.

Naked Exercise #85

Part-Time Jobs, Big-Time Benefits

Think about becoming a Resident Assistant (RA). RAs often get free housing and free food and can make a difference in countless people's lives (that most valuable part of all).

Jobs in college offer it all—money, friends, a social life, and a chance to meet powerful people doing amazing things. Students who work on campus not only earn money to help pay the bills, but they can also find strong connections to campus that can result in better grades and an all-around better experience. For example, working at the information desk in the student union or at the recreational center means meeting people, making friends, knowing about activities on campus, and getting paid. A job in food services can mean catering big events, working with other students, earning money, and often eating for free (or taking home the extras).

When looking for a job, try your best to get a job that can help you further discover your passion. For example, if you love animals, get a job working around animals—not a job in the library.

Brainstorm a list of departments or offices on campus where you think you would like to work. Don't worry if you don't know of any job openings, just write down the jobs or locations that appeal to you the most. You can be the manager of an athletic team, a research assistant to a professor you admire, or wait tables in the campus night spot (yes, some campuses have bars).

Job #1:

Place on campus I might like to work:

_____

Benefits of working here:

_____

_____

_____

How this can help me discover my passion:

_____

_____

_____

Person to contact for more information:

_____

Method to contact this person (face-to-face, Facebook, phone call, etc.):

_____

_____

_____

Job #2:

Place on campus I might like to work:

_____

Benefits of working here:

_____

_____

_____

How this can help me discover my passion:

_____

_____

_____

Person to contact for more information:

_____

Method to contact this person (face-to-face, Facebook, phone call, etc.):

_____

_____

_____

Job #3:

Place on campus I might like to work:

_____

Benefits of working here:

_____

_____

_____

How this can help me discover my passion:

_____

_____

_____

Person to contact for more information:

_____

Method to contact this person (face-to-face, Facebook, phone call, etc.):

_____

_____

_____

   While investigating potential jobs, the Career Center can not only help you find available jobs on or off campus, but they can also help you put together a great resume and develop your interview skills. Begin now by listing the things you have to offer the departments/areas you would like to work for.

What are your strengths related to the job requirements?

_____

_____

_____

What you would like to gain from the experience of working in this department (this will be different for each position you apply for)?

_____

_____

_____

How might this position enhance your college experience?

_____

_____

_____

How does this position relate to your future career goals?

_____

_____

_____

Overall, what can you personally bring to the position and department/office?

_____

_____

_____

What number of hours each week would you like to work (so that you still have time

to do well in your classes)? _____

What hours are you available to work? _____

✎ Naked Journal #85: The Dream Job Interview

Imagine your dream job. Now, locate five people doing what you DREAM to do in life. Contact these people and schedule an interview. (If you don't hear back from the first person, go down your list.) You can explain that you're doing a short paper for a class project. Tell the person you just need five or ten minutes. Schedule a time to interview this person on the phone or in person.

Step 1: Here's what you want to include:

1. What was your dream job when you were younger?

2. What was your first job?

3. What was your biggest break?

4. What has been your greatest professional challenge?

5. What has been your greatest personal challenge?

6. Who are your mentors and how did you find them?

7. What advice would you give to someone who dreams to do what you do?

8. Can I stay in touch with you as I continue on my career path?

9. Ask any question you have: _____

_____

_____

Step 2: Write up the answers and share the answers in a short narrative explaining your experience. Start with how you found the person, how you were able to get an appointment to interview the person, what you learned, what surprised you most, what you took away from this experience.

Step 3: Send a thank-you note to the person (a card).

Naked Exercise #86

Credit Card Use and Abuse

Credit cards aren't dangerous. It's students who abuse them who make them dangerous.

Let's start off with some NAKED true and false questions.

(For this exercise, the suggested background music is the classic song "If I Had a Million Dollars" by Barenaked Ladies.)

1. ALL college students can get a credit card.

True or False

2. Credit cards can be a great way to build credit.

   True or False

3. Credit cards can be a great way to destroy your credit.

   True or False

4. An annual percentage rate is not that important.

   True or False

5. Paying late every month will NOT affect my credit history.

   True or False

6. Spending money I don't have is a good idea.

   True or False

7. Paying the monthly minimum is the fastest way to pay off credit debt.

   True or False

Answer key can be found at the end of this naked exercise, following the naked journal.

Before You Get a Card

Find out the following information:

1. What's the credit limit? _____

2. What's the due date? _____

3. What's the minimum payment? _____

4. What's the late fee? _____

5. Is there an annual fee? _____

6. Will the fees increase? _____

7. What's the interest rate on any unpaid balances? _____

8. Will the interest rate increase (is it an introductory rate)? _____

9. What's the interest rate if you are late paying your balance? _____

10. Is there a rewards program? Will you use the rewards? _____

11. What's the mailing address associated with the account? _____

Time for Your Spending Spree

Ready to go on a spending spree? Now it's time to have some fun and spend irresponsibly. Remember, this is ONLY A WORKBOOK EXERCISE! Do not go out and actually spend money you don't have.

1. You have a credit card with a credit limit of $1,000 and an APR (Annual Percentage Rate) of 19 percent.

2. You know that when the bill comes, you will only have to pay a minimum payment of $40!

3. You decide to enjoy life and use your new card. Go ahead, spend it all (remember, only $40 a month!). Write down what you will buy and do for $1,000.

Desired Item or Fun Experience	Cost
_____	_____
_____	_____
_____	_____
_____	_____
_____	_____
TOTAL	$1,000.00

1. Your bill has arrived! You owe $1,000, but only have to pay $40. However, if you don't pay off the entire amount, you have to pay interest on it for the month.

   If your APR is 19 percent, what is the *monthly* interest rate

   [19 divided by 12 months = _____ percent]?

2. Use this number to calculate the **interest** you owe for the first month

   [_____ percent x $1,000.00 = $_____].

3. Add this to your principal balance of $1,000

   [$_____ + $1,000.00 = $_____] for the **total** you owe.

4. Take this total and subtract your minimum payment of $40

   [$_____ − $40.00 = new balance].

5. Compare your new balance with your original balance and the difference is

   $_____ .

6. Where did the majority of your payment go? _____

7. If you never charged anything else on your credit card again, approximately how long would it take you to pay this off if you only paid the minimum payment each month? _____

Answer key can be found at the end of this naked exercise, following the naked journal.

✎ Naked Journal #86: A Different Kind of Credit Report

Time to find some wisdom. For this journal there are two steps. The first is going to be interviewing a parent, a recent grad, or an adult and asking this person about his or her experience with credit cards.

   Step 1: Here are some questions to ask:

1. When did you get your first card?

2. Why did you decide to get it?

3. How did your parents feel about it (if you told them)?

4. The most irresponsible things you did with your credit card?

5. The most responsible things you did?

6. How it helped you?

7. How it hurt you?

8. What would you do differently if you could do it over again?

9. What advice would you give to college students who get their first credit card?

Step 2: Share your results and write up the results in a short narrative. Make sure to include whom you interviewed.

Answers to NAKED True and False Questions

1. False

2. True

3. True

4. False

5. False

6. False

7. False

Answers to the Credit Card Exercise

1. 1.58 percent monthly percentage rate

2. $15.80 is the interest owed

3. $1,015.80 is your new balance

4. After paying the minimum $40 payment, your remaining balance is $975.80.

5. The difference between your original balance and remaining balance is $24.20.

6. The majority of your payment goes to pay the interest.

7. Just over fourteen years. And you'd pay almost $1,700 in interest along the way.

Naked Exercise #87

Bling and Other Bad Ideas

Ever notice that in music videos, they never show artists getting bills for all the bling? I'd love to see a video that shows an artist spending all his or her money and then getting a bill and having to pay the minimum. It would be fun to see him have to pay the interest on a fifty-carat diamond initial necklace. Now *that* would be entertaining...

Many students find money to be a motivating factor in doing well in college. In other words, graduating, getting a job, and making money can help them buy the things they want. By the time students finally graduate, they've got a diploma *and* a lengthy list of what they plan to spend their paycheck on.

1. What do you want to buy when the money starts rolling (or trickling) in?

_____ Cool car (or any car that runs, to get you to and from work)

_____ House (or loft or condo or igloo)

_____ Furniture

_____ Home theater

_____ Sporting equipment (large, like a boat; smaller, like skis)

_____ Other stuff

2. What experiences do you want to have?

    _____ Dream wedding

    _____ Dream honeymoon

    _____ World travel

    _____ Extreme hobby

    _____ Start your own business

How do you plan to pay for these things or experiences?

_____

_____

How long will it take to earn the money to pay for these things or experiences?

_____

_____

What are you doing now (yes, this very moment) to establish good credit in your name?

_____

_____

What dangerous financial habits do you have that might threaten your credit rating? (Be honest. You can't fix them until you acknowledge them.)

_____

_____

If you are clueless about financial management, what resources exist on or near campus to help you?

_____

_____

✎ Naked Journal #87: Your Most Destructive Habit

What is the one thing you wish you could do differently when it comes to making money, spending money, and managing money? Share the WORST decision you made about managing your money and how this impacted your life. Then figure out what you could have done differently and what you'll do differently the next time around.

Naked Exercise #88

Budgeting and Banking

What do overdraft fees and falling off the top bunk in a dorm room have in common? They both hurt like h*!!.

The best way to keep track of your money is to know how much you're spending on a regular basis. If you don't know how much you're spending, it's easy to spend too much. Sounds simple, right? Well, this actually takes a little work (reminder: that's why it's called a workbook). These days, balancing your budget likely means checking your ATM balance. Unfortunately that little Visa or MasterCard symbol on your debit card can cause problems when it comes to knowing how much you have and don't have.

For example, some places you do business with will put some money aside (that would be _your_ money) to cover themselves in case of certain circumstances. For example, if you get a hotel room (why are you getting a hotel room?!), the hotel could put the total of the room plus $250 aside in case of damages. If you don't cause damage, they will release the funds after you check out. Meanwhile, throughout your stay, you will think you have $250 more in your account than you actually do. So that automatic payment you set up in order to pay with your credit card didn't go through. See where you can run into problems here?

What are the fees if your account is overdrawn? This isn't a rhetorical question. Contact your institution and find out.

Fees associated with a bounced check: _____

_____

    To avoid fees, blemishes, and pimples on your credit, the best bet is to set up a budget. You will always have different needs and activities that require money, so you will want to plan for the unexpected. When you know what you spend, what you owe, and when you owe it, you can keep on top of your money flow.

Total monthly income = _____

Amount	Source
_____	_____
_____	_____
_____	_____
_____	_____

Source of Monthly Expense	Amount	Due Date	Method of Payment
_____	_____	_____	_____
_____	_____	_____	_____
_____	_____	_____	_____
_____	_____	_____	_____
_____	_____	_____	_____
_____	_____	_____	_____
_____	_____	_____	_____
_____	_____	_____	_____
_____	_____	_____	_____

Total cost: _____

Income – Expenses = _____

If you have money left over after you have paid all of your bills and covered your living expenses, what do you do with it?

_____ Put it in savings.

_____ Buy stuff.

_____ Keep it for emergencies.

_____ Pay off debts.

_____ Give it to charity.

_____ Spend it on other people.

If possible, put extra money into a savings account and forget about it.

Why? Things happen. Expenses happen. Emergencies happen. What if your car breaks down? How about an unexpected medical bill? What about an emergency spring break trip to Cancun? (NO, I'm not serious about an emergency spring break trip to Cancun.) But you do need savings in case of an emergency. Owing money that you don't have can be a huge distraction when you are trying to concentrate on classes.

✎ **Naked Journal #88:** Your Relationship with Money

Everyone has a unique relationship with money. How important is money to you? What experiences have you had with money that can illustrate what this relationship means to you? How do you feel about making money? How do you feel about spending it? How do you feel about losing it? What experiences have demonstrated that money can or cannot buy happiness or contentment? What are you likely to truly gain from going after more money? What are you likely to lose or miss out on? If you don't already have thoughts about the importance of money, this will get you thinking about it. You might be surprised to see what you discover.

Naked Exercise #89

Building Good and Bad Credit

Credit is to lenders as hygiene is to potential dates. The better your credit, the more attractive you will be to lenders.

Too many students have NO idea what credit is and why it matters. Instead of telling you why it's so important, I wanted to help you figure it out for yourself. For this exercise, you're going to need to do some work. To help you answer these questions, visit: www.ftc.gov/bcp/edu/pubs/consumer/credit/cre03.shtm

1. A credit score is:

   _____

   _____

2. Having a good credit score is important because:

   _____

   _____

3. Ways I can build good credit:

   _____

   _____

4. Things that will lead me to have bad credit:

   _____

   _____

5. Having a good credit history can help me in the following ways:

   _____

   _____

6. Having bad credit will hurt me in the following ways:

_____

_____

Now that you understand why credit is so important, it's time to put together a plan to build phenomenal credit (or just good credit). For example, if you want to have a credit card, paying the balance in full and on time for the next four years will help you. Having a credit card and NEVER paying the balance on time or not paying it all will hurt you. The goal is to build good credit.

Three things you can do to build the BEST credit:

1. _____

2. _____

3. _____

What are some specific things that you need to stop doing or bad habits related to money that you need to quit in order to avoid financial problems now and in the future?

_____

_____

_____

✎ **Naked Journal #89:** Your Naked Credit Score

Want to know your personal credit score?

Visit www.annualcreditreport.com and get a report for free (this site is the ONLY authorized source for the free annual credit report that is yours by law). What surprised you? What confused you? How were you able to find answers? What can you do to build some credit in the near future?

Naked Exercise #90

Using Your Good and Bad Credit

Now it's time to see just why good credit is so helpful.

Pretend you are buying a new car, a new home, renting an apartment, or attempting to get a credit card. Find out what kind of financing you can get on purchases if your credit score is 575. Then find out what kind of financing you can secure if your credit is 750. To do this, you're going to need to do some research. You can make some calls or send some emails. You can call a bank, call an auto dealer, or contact a credit card company. Mention you're doing a project for school about the importance of credit scores. Then explain that you want to know how credit scores impact obtaining loans. If you're calling an auto dealer, ask about financing a car. If you're calling a bank, ask about financing a home purchase. If you're calling a credit card company, ask about getting a card. WARNING: DO NOT ACTUALLY GET THE CAR, HOME, OR LOAN. This is purely for research. This is NOT REAL!!! Please don't send me an email telling me you bought a three-bedroom house for no money down. That's NOT what this is about. Complete the following information during your call:

1. Whom did you contact?

_____

_____

2. What did you inquire about buying?

_____

_____

3. What credit score do you need to get a loan (or financing)?

_____

_____

4. What's your interest rate with a score of 575?

_____

_____

5. What would be your interest rate with a score of 750?

_____

_____

Share the story of what you investigated purchasing and what you discovered about having good or bad credit.

✎ Naked Journal #90: Credit Mysteries Revealed

Talk to your parents or relatives and ask them to share a tip and story about what it means to have a credit score. Ask them to share the story of the first time they realized a credit score mattered. What were they buying? Why did their credit score matter? What happened as a result of the score?

HOOKING UP, RELATIONSHIPS, SEX/NO SEX, DRINKING, DRUGS, MENTAL HEALTH, AND MORE...

A Short Note before the Self-Exam

You've reached the dating, relationship, sex, drinking, and drugs section. (I know that's really all you wanted.) If you're looking for advice about money, dating, sex, hooking up, drinking, drugs, mental health issues, and more, *The Naked Roommate* book is the place to go. For the workbook, I wanted to take some time to focus on mistakes and regrets. I hand-picked the most common issues and created Naked Exercises to help you out. If you need more answers, please visit me...

ONLINE: www.TheNakedRoommate.com
FACEBOOK: www.Facebook.com/TNRFanPage
TWITTER: @Harlan Cohen, @NakedRoommate
YOUTUBE: www.YouTube.com/harlancohendotcom

Rate using a scale of 1–10.

> **1** = Not true → **5** = Somewhat true → **10** = Doesn't get any truer

_____ I'm worried about finding a date in college.

_____ I have a hard time rejecting people who like me.

_____ I think a one-night stand sounds like fun.

_____ I've never been in a relationship before.

_____ I'm waiting to have sex until I get married.

_____ I'm aware that approximately one in four college-age students has HPV (the virus that causes genital warts).

_____ I'm aware that one in four students has genital herpes.

_____ I'm sick over my long-distance relationship.

_____ Having sex with multiple partners will give me a good reputation.

_____ I don't have time to date in college.

_____ I'm nervous that I'll be pressured to have sex in college.

_____ I'm looking forward to casually dating lots of people, just to get to know them.

_____ If you love someone and want a committed relationship, it's important to have sex with them.

_____ Like my Facebook status says, I'm looking for whatever I can get.

_____ I plan to make sure that my roommate never has sex in our room.

Naked Exercise #91

The College Hookup

If you're looking for something noncommittal, ambiguous, and uncomfortable, hooking up is the perfect love—I mean lust—connection.

Hooking up is one of the most common ways college students find love or lust. Unlike the high school hookup, the college hookup can be more intense. Meaning, there are more opportunities to be in more rooms with more people and the people in these rooms are willing to go further sexually. This also means you have the opportunity to do things that you might ultimately regret. I know the hookup sounds like fun, but once the itching, burning, and pregnancy test come in, the fun will be done.

Here's a list of various college hookups. Think about what you would be willing or not willing to do.

Type of Hookup	Would Be OK Doing It
(Check out Tip #55 in *The Naked Roommate* for the definition of each type of hookup.)	
The Drunk Hookup	_____
The Friendly Hookup	_____
The Rebound Hookup	_____
The Cheating Hookup	_____
The Desperation Hookup	_____
The Online Hookup	_____
The Who's Next Hookup	_____

Type of Hookup	Would Be OK Doing It
The Ex Hookup	_____
The Visitor Hookup	_____
The I Love You Hookup	_____
The Convenience Hookup	_____
The First Week Hookup	_____
The Just Want to Have Fun Hookup	_____
The Weekend Hookup	_____
The Sympathy Hookup	_____
The Help Me Hookup	_____
The Repeat Backup Hookup	_____

First, let's look at the not-so-good part of hooking up. What are five risks that come with hooking up? Use the previous list to name the type of hookup and the not-so-good outcome that can result from it.

Example:

Name of Hookup: _The Drunk Hookup_

Danger/risk: _I end up in a situation that goes too far because I'm not thinking clearly._

1. Name of Hookup: _____

Danger/risk: _____

_____

_____

2. Name of Hookup: _____

Danger/risk: _____

_____

_____

3. Name of Hookup: _____

Danger/risk: _____

_____

_____

4. Name of Hookup: _____

Danger/risk: _____

_____

_____

5. Name of Hookup: _____

Danger/risk: _____

_____

_____

Now, in all fairness it's important to focus on the positive parts of hooking up. What are five benefits/rewards that come with hooking up?

Example:

Name of Hookup: The First Week Hookup _____

Benefit: I can get to know someone quickly that I wouldn't have known otherwise.

1. Name of Hookup: _____

Benefit: _____

_____

_____

2. Name of Hookup: _____

Benefit: _____

_____

_____

3. Name of Hookup: _____

Benefit: _____

_____

_____

4. Name of Hookup: _____

Benefit: _____

_____

_____

5. Name of Hookup: _____

Benefit: _____

_____

_____

Now, how can someone get those same benefits without hooking up?

For example: _If the benefit of the First Week Hookup is getting to know someone quickly, an alternative way could be to go to a floor event in my residence hall or sit down and share a meal with someone who interests me._

1. Benefit: _____

Alternative way to get the same result(s): _____

_____

_____

2. Benefit: _____

Alternative way to get the same result(s): _____

_____

_____

3. Benefit: _____

Alternative way to get the same result(s): _____

_____

_____

Question to think about: Why do you think so many college students prefer hooking up as opposed to dating? What makes hooking up easier than dating? What makes dating easier than hooking up? There is no right answer—it's just your opinion:

_____

_____

✎ **Naked Journal #91:** The Hookup Exposed

Do you think the hookup culture in college is a good thing or a bad thing? When writing your essay, draw on personal experiences from your own life or the life of your friends (no names please). You can use the answers in this exercise to support your point of view. Make sure to include at least two stories to support your opinion. There are no right answers—it's just how you feel.

Naked Exercise #92

The Long-Distance Relationship

If you do the LDR, make sure to HALOYR (Have a Life Outside Your Relationship). Being miserable isn't a sign of being devoted; it's a sign of being in a miserable relationship.

So you're in a relationship and you want to keep it going, but the love of your life will be far away from you. Everyone tells you to end it NOW! (Not me.) But do you want to know how to keep it going? Here are some yes or no questions and a worksheet to help you find your own answers. Soon, you will know whether or not this LDR will last.

1. Having fun without my significant other means there is something wrong with my long-distance relationship.

    YES / NO

2. My significant other discourages me from getting involved on campus and discourages me from making new friends.

    YES / NO

3. My significant other often accuses me of getting too close to members of the opposite sex and is frequently jealous.

    YES / NO

4. I spend at least one hour a day on the phone, texting, or communicating with my significant other.

YES / NO

5. I leave campus more than once a month to spend time with my significant other.

YES / NO

6. I'm afraid my significant other is cheating on me.

YES / NO

7. I often think that having a long-distance relationship is a mistake.

YES / NO

8. I spend at least two weekends a month with my significant other.

YES / NO

9. I find it hard to be involved in clubs and organizations and have a significant other because it's too hard to balance my time.

YES / NO

10. More than one friend or family member has told me they think my long-distance relationship is unhealthy.

YES / NO

Answer key to the LDR Questionnaire can be found on page 308.

Why do you and your long-distance partner want to keep this relationship going?

_____

_____

_____

What do you have to gain by staying together (the pros)?

_____

_____

_____

How much time do you spend each week communicating with him or her?

_____

Are you completely committed to staying in this relationship or will you end it should you find someone else whom you find attractive and interesting to date?

_____

_____

_____

Are you open to meeting new people, making new friends, and possibly a new romantic partner?

_____

_____

_____

In what ways is your long-distance relationship limiting your current college experience?

_____

_____

_____

Do you believe that your long-distance partner is being completely faithful?

_____

_____

_____

Do you think that he or she is limiting his or her social interactions and potential to meet a new partner to the same extent you are?

_____

_____

_____

In what ways can you tell that your long-distance relationship is growing and maturing?

_____

_____

_____

How prepared are you if your long-distance partner ends the relationship?

_____

_____

_____

Answers to the LDR Questionnaire

If you answered YES to three or more questions, YES your LDR is in big trouble. Here's why:

1. You should ALWAYS be able to have fun with and without your significant other. Having fun apart is a sign that you are a fun person—not a disloyal partner.

2. Your significant other should want you to get involved on campus. The risk is that you'll meet someone else. Pressuring you to avoid having a life on campus is the worst possible relationship.

3. Jealousy is poison to a long-distance relationship. If you have a trusting, loving relationship, there shouldn't be jealousy.

4. Spending an hour a day means NOT spending an hour a day connecting to people on campus. You need a life outside your LDR to make your LDR survive.

5. You can't find connections, find friends, and have a life on campus if you're never on campus!

6. If you're afraid your significant other is cheating, you don't trust your significant other. And that's a doomed relationship.

7. If you think an LDR is a mistake, it is 100 percent a mistake. Visit the risk-taking exercise and break up!

8. Spending half the month with your boyfriend or girlfriend will keep you from making other friends—boys and girls.

9. If you can't get involved in clubs and organizations because your relationship takes up too much time, it's taking up too much time.

10. If the people who love you the most think the relationship is bad, it's BAD!

✎ Naked Journal #92: LDR Fears

What are your five biggest fears when it comes to attempting to have a long-distance relationship? Once you've written out your biggest fears, write down how you will address each of these fears with your partner. If you can't work out these fears now, you have good reason to be afraid because LDRs will not get easier with distance or time.

Naked Exercise #93

Demanding and Commanding Respect

Want to know if you're with your very best choice and NOT just your only choice? Answer this question:

If you knew at all times that you had one thousand people who wanted to date you, love you, and respect you, would you ever put up with someone who treated you poorly, disrespected you, didn't return your calls, verbally abused you, hit you, alienated you, said terrible things about your family, or made you feel anything less than attractive?

Your answer: _____

What are ten things you will *never* put up with in a relationship?

1. _____

2. _____

3. _____

4. _____

5. _____

6. _____

7. _____

8. _____

9. _____

10. _____

To avoid regrets in the world of love (or lust), you need to always know that you live in a world of options. The more you can be reminded that you have options, the less likely you are to EVER put up with garbage. Start with a promise to yourself. Save this just in case you ever have to face a breakup.

I (fill in your name) _____ know that I live in a world of options. When someone treats me poorly or disrespects me, I know that there are thousands of people who can date me.

I can always look for people to date in the following places:

1. _____

2. _____

3. _____

4. _____

5. _____

When I'm single, these are ten things that I can do to pass the time:

1. _____

2. _____

3. _____

4. _____

5. _____

6. _____

7. _____

8. _____

9. _____

10. _____

When I'm single, these are five people I can hang out with:

1. _____

2. _____

3. _____

4. _____

5. _____

Should anyone ever pressure me to do something that I don't want to do or treat me poorly, here's what I will say to myself:

_____

_____

_____

Should anyone ever pressure me to do something that I don't want to do, here's what I will say to the person:

_____

_____

_____

What I love/like about my significant other:

_____

_____

_____

What I'm afraid I will miss out on in college if we stay together:

_____

_____

_____

Ways I can have a life on campus and still have a relationship with my boyfriend or girlfriend at home:

_____

_____

_____

✎ **Naked Journal #93:** Demanding and Commanding Respect

Think about your relationships with your friends. Now think about your past or present relationships with a significant other. How have you been disrespected in the past or the present? What did you do when you were disrespected? Did you say what you felt? Did you keep your feelings a secret? Share the story of when you were disrespected and how you demanded respect or kept your feelings a secret and allowed someone to disrespect you. Share what happened before, during, and after. If you haven't been able to demand respect, share what you will do the next time this happens so it will NEVER happen again.

Naked Exercise #94

I Got Dumped and No Longer Have a Relationship

Breaking up might be sad for you, but it's a great moment for all those other people waiting to date you.

Hooking up, dating, and being in love are the best parts of a relationship. The falling out of love, getting cheated on, or getting broken up with parts are the worst (can't see you arguing with that).

When it happens, there's a mix of anger, resentment, hurt, confusion, and disappointment. Often times, getting broken up with can leave you feeling broken, ugly, and unattractive. Before you feel like it's hopeless, here's a little Naked Exercise to help you gain some composure and move on. Give yourself time to experience the following phases. Feel free to whip out your *Naked Roommate* book for more (see the six phases of survival described in Tip #64 in *The Naked Roommate*).

Phase 1: Get Upset and Get Angry

Get in touch with your feelings! What upset you about the breakup? Use this space to feel hurt, confused, and vent.

_____

_____

_____

_____

_____

_____

_____

Phase 2: Know That You're Still Desirable (aka on Fire, Hottt)

You are incredibly attractive. NEVER FORGET IT! What qualities do you focus on in yourself to remember what an amazing person you are?

_____   _____

_____   _____

_____   _____

Phase 3: Surround Yourself with Friends and Activities

Who are your greatest supporters and sources of comfort?

_____   _____

_____   _____

_____   _____

What are your favorite activities that can keep you busy?

_____   _____

_____   _____

_____   _____

Phase 4: Consider a Break from Dating

Remember that you ALWAYS live in a world of options. Discuss why a break is important, what you've learned, and how a break can help you through the difficult time.

_____

_____

_____

_____

_____

_____

Phase 5: Avoid Running Right Back to an Ex
Write down every reason that this would be a very bad idea.

_____

_____

_____

_____

_____

Phase 6: Get Back Out There
What would be your preferred way(s) to begin meeting people again?

_____

_____

_____

_____

_____

_____

Keep this handy in case you ever need it. It shows your strength and ability to get through the sting of a breakup. It's always good to be prepared.

NOTE: If you find all of this too hard, get professional support (from a therapist, counselor, or psychiatrist).

✎ **Naked Journal #94:** Healing a Broken Heart

Have you ever experienced a difficult breakup? Write how you coped the first time you were brokenhearted. What was the hardest part? How did you get over it? What helped you heal the most? Explain how you grew stronger having gone through the breakup experience. If you haven't gone through a difficult breakup, find someone in your circle of friends who has gone through this and share his or her story (change the names to protect the innocent, please).

Naked Exercise #95

Deciding to Do It or NOT Do It

Make sure you know the person you're getting into or who's getting into you. Once you do it, you can't undo it. If you don't want to do it, there are a lot of other things you can do.

Having sex is one of the biggest decisions you'll make in college (after choosing a major). It's emotional. It's physical. It can have a lifelong impact (can you say "pregnancy scare"?). Unlike your major, once you have sex you can't switch back to being a virgin (or take back the sex). And beyond the flood of emotions, you have the risk of sexual souvenirs (herpes, genital warts, chlamydia, etc.), pregnancy (that dorm room can get very small with a crib), and reputations. Before getting into the sex part of this exercise, I want to take a second to do a virgin exercise. You can be a virgin, date, hook up, and have a close relationship. NOT EVERYONE wants sex. If you are a virgin, answer the following questions:

1. Why is your virginity important to you?

   _____

2. How long are you waiting to have sex?

   _____

3. Is this negotiable? What would change your mind?

_____

_____

_____

4. Is there a club or organization on campus where you can meet people with similar values?

_____

_____

_____

5. How will you tell someone you date that you are waiting?

_____

_____

_____

6. What are the five biggest myths about virgins (you can share this with your partner after you tell him or her you're waiting)?

a. _____

b. _____

c. _____

d. _____

e. _____

Now on to the Sex...

For your convenience, I've copied parts of the Virgin Questionnaire (with a few extra items thrown in) from Tip #65 from *The Naked Roommate* and put it here to make it easier for you to answer and refer to later (when you may really need it). And don't worry that it's called the Virgin Questionnaire; this works for virgins and anyone having sex.

Answer each of the following honestly and just for yourself before allowing someone to get in touch with you and your body.

1. Are you 100 percent sure you want to have sex with this person?   YES / NO

Why are you so sure or unsure?

_____

_____

2. Can you openly communicate with your sex partner before,
    during, and after sex?   YES / NO

What gives you this feeling?

_____

_____

3. Have you asked this person if he or she has been tested for
    herpes, genital warts, HIV, chlamydia, human papillomavirus
    (the virus that causes genital warts), or other sexual souvenirs?   YES / NO

How can you be sure? Did you or your partner get tested?

_____

_____

4. Do you have contraception (condoms, birth control, etc.)?   YES / NO

If your partner says she's on birth control pills/has a diaphragm/has an IUD, how can you be so sure?

_____

_____

5. Have you discussed what you would do if this sex
    resulted in a pregnancy?   YES / NO

What would you do? What would your partner do?

_____

_____

6. Have you or your partner pressured the other to have sex?   YES / NO

If the answer is YES, in what way could this possibly be OK?

_____

_____

7. Are you planning on having sex for the first time
    completely sober?   YES / NO

If the answer is NO, how could this be OK?

_____

_____

8. Does this decision (to have sex) work with your faith?   YES / NO

If not, how will you make this compatible?

_____

_____

9. Is there a chance that it would be awkward to see
    the person the next day?   YES / NO

If it might be awkward, how could this be the right thing to do?

_____

_____

10. Do you have a comfortable place to have sex (that's not
    where your roommate sleeps in the next bed over)?   YES / NO

Where is the ideal (and realistic) place that you could be intimate with someone?

_____

_____

11. Does it feel 100 percent right for you?   YES / NO

12. Do you know the person's first and last name?   YES / NO

13. Can you pronounce and spell his or her name?   YES / NO

What else is important to know about the person you are having sex with? List
everything else that is essential for you to have sex.

_____

_____

_____

**If you can't talk about these things with the other person, keep your
pants on.**
Since you probably won't have this questionnaire with you when the time comes
to decide whether or not to have sex with someone, answering the questions now
will help you mentally prepare. The point is to know yourself and prepare to make
the choices that are right for you, even in the face of strong temptation. There are
few things worse than having sex and then regretting it.

Naked Journal #95: Sex in College

What has surprised you most about people's perspectives on having sex in college? What has surprised you about how other people view and use sex in college? How has this impacted you and the choices you make and how you see the people around you? When sharing your feelings, do not identify people by name. Feel free to make up names to protect the innocent.

Designated Doodle Space

Suggested doodle: please keep it clean...

Naked Self-Exam Thirteen

Drinking and Drugs

Rate using a scale of 1–10.

> **1** = Not true → **5** = Somewhat true → **10** = Doesn't get any truer

_____ I drink when I party because it's what makes it fun.

_____ I don't drink.

_____ I drink because it's expected in college.

_____ I know my limit when drinking.

_____ Once I start drinking, I can quickly get out of control and drink too much.

_____ I often don't remember what I did or said when I was drinking.

_____ I have had unplanned sex when drunk.

_____ I can rely on my friends to look out for me when I'm drinking.

_____ I know at least one person who has had something scary happen to them because of drinking.

_____ I have driven a car when under the influence of alcohol.

_____ I sometimes drink when I'm by myself.

_____ I know at least one person who smokes pot.

_____ I would not be able to recognize the smell of pot if I encountered it.

_____ It doesn't bother me to be around people doing drugs.

_____ If I saw people taking drugs at a party, I would leave immediately.

_____ I have never seen drugs on campus.

_____ Smoking is a good alternative to drinking or taking drugs.

_____ I think the negative hype about drugs being a problem is overrated.

_____ I would never try drugs because I fear becoming addicted or dying.

_____ I have no problem saying NO to alcohol and drugs.

NAKED ALERT:

**If you are not of legal drinking age
you should NOT be drinking alcohol!!!!
That said (and yes I had to put this in here),
some students will choose to illegally drink.**

Naked Exercise #96

An Alcohol Examination

Most students think they know more than they actually know when it comes to alcohol use and abuse. But most don't know as much as they think they know.

Welcome to the Alcohol Examination. Please put all beverages down. This exercise should be done while completely sober. (If you're too drunk to do this Naked Exercise or you spill alcohol on this page, flip to the Naked Exercise about alcohol addiction because you might be in serious trouble!)

Let's start out with some multiple-choice questions.

Multiple-Choice

1. What percentage of college students do you think reported drinking alcohol within the past thirty days:

   a. 45.7 percent

   b. 65.9 percent

   c. 72 percent

   d. 82.1 percent

   e. 93 percent

2. A man and woman both have one alcoholic beverage. In general, a woman metabolizes alcohol at a rate

   a. slower than a man

   b. same as a man

   c. faster than a man

3. Which of the following does the term "one drink" refer to?

   a. 12 fl. oz. of regular beer (about 5 percent alcohol)

   b. 8–9 fl. oz. of malt liquor (about 7 percent alcohol)

   c. Whatever someone pours into your glass

   d. One pitcher of alcoholic beverage

   e. The amount dispensed in a keg stand

   f. 5 fl. oz. of table wine (about 12 percent alcohol)

   g. 1.5 fl. oz. shot of 80-proof spirits ("hard liquor"—whiskey, gin, rum, vodka, tequila, etc.) about 40 percent alcohol

   h. 12 oz. cup of fruit punch at a party

4. The National Institute of Alcohol Abuse and Alcoholism defines binge drinking as a pattern of drinking that brings a person's blood alcohol concentration (BAC) to 0.08 percent or above. This typically happens when men consume five or more drinks, and when women consume four or more drinks in a time span of

    a. one hour

    b. two hours

    c. three hours

    d. four hours

    e. five hours

True or False

College students reported doing the following most of the time or always when partying over the course of a year:

1. 29.6 percent of students alternate alcoholic and non-alcoholic beverages while partying.

    True or False

2. 39.9 percent of students avoid drinking games.

    True or False

3. 23.2 percent of students choose not to drink alcohol.

    True or False

4. 38.2 percent of students determine in advance not to exceed a predetermined number of drinks when partying.

    True or False

5. 78 percent of students eat something before partying.

    True or False

6. 34.5 percent of students will have a friend tell them when they have had enough to drink.

   True or False

7. 66.3 percent of students keep track of how many drinks they consumed.

   True or False

8. 30.6 percent of students will drink one or fewer drinks per hour.

   True or False

9. 84.9 percent of students will stay with the same set of friends the entire time drinking.

   True or False

10. 82.9 percent of students will use a designated driver.

    True or False

11. 34.6 percent of students who drank alcohol did something they later regretted.

    True or False

12. 30.4 percent of students who drank alcohol forgot where they were or what they did.

    True or False

13. 16.5 percent of students who drank alcohol had unprotected sex.

    True or False

14. 14.9 percent of students who drank alcohol were physically injured.

    True or False

Answers to the Alcohol Examination

1. Did you guess **e)** 93 percent? If you did, you would be like most college students—WRONG! The answer is 65.9 percent of students reported having NO drinks over a span of thirty days. The reality is that most students perceived the answer to be 93 percent. The truth is, the amount of people you think are drinking is not even close to the actual number of people drinking.

2. If you answered **c)**, at a faster rate than a man, you are CORRECT! Women absorb and metabolize alcohol differently than men. In general, women have less body water than men of similar body weight, so that women achieve higher concentrations of alcohol in the blood after drinking equivalent amounts of alcohol. In addition, women appear to eliminate alcohol from the blood faster than men. This finding may be explained by women's higher liver volume per unit lean body mass because alcohol is metabolized almost entirely in the liver. (Source: http://pubs.niaaa.nih.gov/publications/aa46.htm)

3. One drink refers to **a)** 12 fl. oz. of regular beer (about 5 percent alcohol), **b)** 8–9 fl. oz. of malt liquor (about 7 percent alcohol), **f)** 5 fl. oz. of table wine (about 12 percent alcohol), **g)** 1.5 fl. oz. shot of 80-proof spirits ("hard liquor"—whiskey, gin, rum, vodka, tequila, etc.—about 40 percent alcohol). IT DOES NOT REFER TO
    c. whatever someone pours into your glass
    d. one pitcher of alcoholic beverage
    e. the amount dispensed in a keg stand
    h. 12 oz. cup of fruit punch at a party (who knows what the hell is in there!)

4. If you answered two hours, you are correct! This can vary based on body weight and the amount of food in the person's stomach. The general rule is to limit alcohol consumption to one drink an hour.

True or False: If you guessed every single answer is TRUE, you just got them all correct. If you guessed they were all false, you should speak to an alcohol and drug counselor ASAP. Put down your drink and run (or walk if running is too hard). How did you do it? You must be really lucky or naturally brilliant!

Source: American College Health Assessment / National College Health Assessment Spring 2011

Now Take a Look Back at the Exam Questions

List the questions you got wrong. What surprised you about each answer? How will knowing this information impact you?

1. _____

_____

_____

_____

2. _____

_____

_____

_____

3. _____

_____

_____

_____

List three questions you got correct that might have surprised you as well, and how knowing this information will impact your behavior on campus.

1. _____

_____

_____

2. _____

_____

_____

_____

3. _____

_____

_____

_____

✎ Naked Journal #96: Alcohol Answers

What questions do you have about alcohol use and abuse in college? Write them down. Make sure you have at least ten. Then find the answers. This is your time to ask yourself questions and get the answers you need. If you're not sure of the answer to your question, talk to friends, student leaders on campus you respect, or professionals. Sample question: Why do guys think it's cool to get drunk and hit on girls? Answer: They don't have the courage to take risks sober because they can't handle rejection!

Naked Exercise #97

Alcohol: The Social Lubricant

Put people in a room with alcohol and they will often talk more, hook up more, and vomit on each other more (no, none of this is a good thing or the only way to meet, talk, and vomit).

You already know that drinking in college can be a problem. But yet, so many brilliant (and not-so-brilliant) students drink. After answering the quiz in the previous exercise, you now know that not as many people on campus are drinking as most students think. A lot of students DO NOT drink at all.

So here's the big question—why do so many students engage in unhealthy drinking? I have my thoughts (check out *The Naked Roommate*), but this is the place for you to take a second to think about the WHY behind college drinking. This doesn't have to be about why you drink or don't drink. It's a general question.

List Five Reasons You Think College Students Drink

(And you are NOT allowed to list having fun as one reason. I'm looking for something deeper. Think about what makes it fun. What does drinking allow people to do that they have a hard time doing while totally sober?)

Reason #1:

_____

_____

Reason #2:

_____

_____

Reason #3:

_____

_____

Reason #4:

_____

_____

Reason #5:

_____

_____

For all these reasons, could someone engage in a different kind of behavior to get the same benefits?

1. _____

_____

2. _____

_____

3. _____

_____

4. _____

_____

5. _____

_____

If there's NO WAY to get the same benefit without drinking, please explain.

_____

_____

_____

✎ **Naked Journal #97:** Why Do College Students Drink?
Why do you do what you do? Why do you drink? Why don't you drink? What has influenced your decision? Write a note to yourself sharing your belief system when it comes to using or not using alcohol. Hang onto this. It will be interesting to see how your view has changed over the course of your college experience.

Naked Exercise #98

Deciding to Drink Alcohol or Milk

Drunk people say and do stupid things. They are often just too drunk to remember (unless you record it for them on your phone and play it back in the morning).

The best way to avoid being a stupid drunk, getting arrested, and doing things you regret while drinking is to NOT drink. If you don't want to drink, you don't have to drink. A lot of students aren't drinking. They just aren't talking about it. The challenge for a lot of college students is that being sober means having to take social and emotional risks without being wasted. The hard part is that if the emotional or social risk doesn't go as planned, these students will find it too embarrassing or upsetting to take future risks. That's where getting drunk helps. But it's not a fix. It's just a temporary way to fix a deeper problem. If this describes you, turn back to the risk-taking exercise earlier in the book and use this as your guide to taking risks while sober.

So how do you avoid the whole stupid drunk thing, even when out with friends? For the sake of this exercise, list five things you can do to avoid alcohol or drugs if someone offers them to you. How can you respond and not be uncomfortable?

1. Hold on to the same drink the whole night (without drinking it).

2. _____

3. _____

4. _____

5. _____

What are the three stupidest things you've ever seen someone do or say while drunk (feel free to talk about yourself as a good friend if you don't want anyone to see this)?

1. _____

_____

2. _____

_____

3. _____

_____

What were the consequences of these three stupidest things you've seen someone say or do while drunk? Did someone get expelled, fired, arrested, thrown off campus, broken up with, buried…?

1. _____

_____

2. _____

_____

3. _____

_____

The Power of Options

Remember earlier in the workbook when I talked about options? The more options you have, the easier it is to avoid uncomfortable situations. When you have options (other friends, other places on campus, other interests), you can avoid dangerous situations.

Imagine you are in a situation where someone is pressuring you to do something you don't feel comfortable doing. What would you say to the person or people? Write it here so you will always be ready to say it should you feel it.

_____

_____

Imagine you are in a situation where you witness someone else being pressured to do something dangerous or stupid. What would you say to the person or people pressuring this person? Write it here so you will always be ready to say it should you feel it.

_____

_____

✎ Naked Journal #98: Alcohol Tragedies

It's time to whip out that computer and do some research. Your task is to find three articles about three incidents in the past three years where college students have been negatively impacted by alcohol. This can be on campus, around campus, or somewhere in the country. You can search the college newspaper, the local newspaper, Google news, or any other news source. Summarize the three stories in a short paper and share what you have learned from this journal entry.

Naked Exercise #99

Drinking and Driving Never Mix

Driving after drinking ONE alcoholic beverage is driving under the influence.

If you plan to drink—even just occasionally—know your resources and be ready to use them. There is NO excuse to EVER drive drunk. There is NEVER a reason to get behind the wheel or sit in the car of someone who is driving drunk.

We all know this, but yet, so many people still get in the car. Why do you think it's so hard for students to avoid cars when drinking?

_____

_____

_____

Should you be in a situation where someone under the influence wants to drive you or him or herself, what can you do or say to help?

_____

_____

_____

If someone drives under the influence and refuses to listen to you, is it OK to call the police and make an anonymous report? Please explain your answer:

_____

_____

_____

Need a Ride? Here Ya Go!

Campus-Based Taxi Service

Does your campus have a student-run service for people who drink? _____

If so, write their contact number here: _____

Days and hours of operation: _____

Local Bus Service

Cost: _____

Bus stops near where you party: _____

Hours of operation: _____

Taxi Services in the Area

Name and phone number: _____

Name and phone number: _____

Hospitals Near Campus

Name and address: _____

Name and address: _____

Attorneys and Campus Resources Specializing in Alcohol-Related Offenses

Contact name: _____

Contact number: _____

NOTE: Just because there are places to party—close to home or otherwise—if you are under twenty-one and you get caught drinking or in possession of alcohol, you could get arrested. If you do get busted, don't keep it a secret. Talk to your parents and get help. Not getting help is being VERY stupid.

✎ Naked Journal #99: Sober Driving

Describe a situation where you (or a friend) drove under the influence or a situation where someone driving you was under the influence. How did you get into this situation? How did you handle this? What was the hardest part of the situation? How did you resolve it? What would you do differently? What was the short-term outcome? What was the long-term outcome? If this has never happened to you, find someone it has happened to and ask them these questions.

Naked Exercise #100

You Might Have an Alcohol Problem If...

If the people who love you the most are worried that you have a drinking problem, you already have a drinking problem.

When Does Casual Drinking Become an Addiction?

Addiction is a chronic, progressive, relapsing disorder characterized by compulsive use of one or more substances that results in physical, psychological, or social harm to the individual and continued use of the substance or substances despite this harm. Addiction has two possible components: physical dependence and psychological dependence.

- **Physical dependence**—a state of becoming physically adapted to alcohol or other drugs. There are two important aspects to physical dependence:
  - **Tolerance**—the need for higher and higher doses to achieve the same effects.
  - **Withdrawal**—the appearance of physical symptoms (e.g., nausea, chills, and vomiting) when someone stops taking a drug too quickly.
- **Psychological dependence**—a subjective sense or need for alcohol or other drugs, either for its positive effects or to avoid negative effects associated with no use.

Source: www.dol.gov/aso/programs/drugs/workingpartners/sab/addiction.asp

Please answer the following questions about alcohol dependence. You don't have to show them to anyone but yourself. But if they lead to a scary conclusion, you need to use them to motivate you to change and get some help. Smart, talented, and brilliant students can find themselves powerless to alcohol and other addiction. Regaining the power begins with acknowledging the truth that you need help.

1. Do you drink more than you plan on drinking in one sitting?   YES / NO

If you answered YES, why do you think you drink more than you plan on drinking?

_____

_____

2. Have you ever felt you should cut down on your drinking?   YES / NO

If you answered YES, when and why did you think this at the time?

_____

_____

3. Have people annoyed you by criticizing your drinking?   YES / NO

If you answered YES, what have they said to you?

_____

_____

4. Have you ever felt bad, guilty, or regretful about your drinking?   YES / NO

If you answered YES, what did you do to bring about these feelings?

_____

_____

5. Do you drink alone?   YES / NO

If you answered YES, why do you think this is normal and/or acceptable?

_____

_____

6. Do you drink to avoid dealing with your worries and concerns?   YES / NO

If you answered YES, why do you think this is normal and/or acceptable?

_____

_____

7. Has drinking affected your reputation?   YES / NO

If you answered YES, why do you think this is normal and/or acceptable?

_____

_____

8. Has drinking resulted in your missing class or work?   YES / NO

If you answered YES, why do you think this is normal and/or acceptable?

_____

_____

9. Have you ever been written up, arrested, injured,
    or hospitalized as a result of your drinking?   YES / NO

If you answered YES, why do you think this is normal and/or acceptable?

_____

_____

10. Have you ever had a drink first thing in the morning
    to steady your nerves or to get rid of a hangover?   YES / NO

If you answered YES, do you believe this to be normal and/or acceptable?

_____

_____

11. Have you ever lied about your drinking?   YES / NO

If you answered YES, do you believe this to be normal and/or acceptable?

_____

_____

12. Does anyone in your family have a history of alcohol use or abuse?   YES / NO

If you answered YES, why is this important to know?

_____

_____

Did you answer YES to two of these questions? If so, you may have a drinking problem. Please get help.

Where to Get Help

Counseling centers, local hospitals, addiction specialists, therapists, group therapy, and doctors are all places to seek help. List at least one place you can turn to for help.

Contact name: _____

Phone number: _____

Address: _____

✎ Naked Journal #100: A Brush with Alcohol

Share how alcohol addiction has impacted your life. It can be yours, a significant other's, a loved one's, a sibling's, a parent's, or a family member's. How did the problem begin? How did it develop? What incidents impacted you? How were you able to deal with this? How did you get support? If you still need help, where can you get the help you need to come to terms with this behavior? (If you truly do not know anyone with an alcohol addiction, seek out a fellow student who does for help with these questions.)

Naked Exercise #101

Drugs on Campus

Today, drugs are more accessible, more easily consumed, and more dangerous. If you're going to be stupid, don't kill yourself.

All the exercises about alcohol can also be applied to drugs. In fact, alcohol is just one of the drugs (the most commonly used drug) that's going to be in your path in college. But if you want to find more drugs, they are out there and available. When you do make this decision, appreciate a few things. And they are surrounded by myths—myths that can be dangerous if you don't know the truth.

Myth #1: Hanging Out with People Who Do Drugs Will Have NO Impact on You

Think about all the ways that the people around you influence your behavior. Which of the following have you done? Check those that apply to you:

_____ Eaten less because I was with people who weren't eating much.

_____ Eaten beyond being full since everyone around was eating and eating.

_____ Exercised longer and harder when working out at a busy gym.

_____ Blew off exercising because I was hanging out with people who weren't interested in working out.

_____ Watched a movie I hated because the group wanted to see it.

_____ Studied longer and more seriously to keep up with my study group.

_____ Let others convince me not to study.

_____ Drank when I wasn't in the mood because everyone was drinking.

_____ Had sex with someone who really wanted to, even though I didn't.

If you checked even one of these, your behavior has been impacted by what someone else does or wants you to do. It is normal (so you're not the only sheep in the bunch), but it can be dangerous too. Being in a room with people who do drugs will make it easier to do drugs. It's just that simple.

If someone offered you drugs and you didn't want to participate, what would you do? What would you say? How would you say it? Well, there are two responses to this question. The person who has ONE group of friends has a harder time saying NO when faced with this question. BUT the person who lives in a world of options and has more than one group of friends can be honest because he or she always has different choices available.

Assuming you don't want to do drugs, what will you say when someone offers them to you?

_____

_____

_____

_____

If your friends reject you because you don't want to do drugs, where can you find more friends that share your belief system?

Club/Activity/Organization: _____

Club/Activity/Organization: _____

Club/Activity/Organization: _____

Myth #2: Drugs Are Safe

I know you are sure that drugs are safe, but unless you've made it or grown it, you have no idea who has handled it. For this exercise, track the path of a vegetable from the fields to the grocery store at the local market. List all the people who touch the tomato, cucumber, or favorite veggie you eat in your salad. Do some research here:

Location 1: The Farm _____

Who potentially touched your vegetable?

A farm worker with dirty fingernails and a bad stomach flu.

Location 2: _____

Who potentially touched your vegetable?

_____

Location 3: _____

Who potentially touched your vegetable?

_____

Location 4: _____

Who potentially touched your vegetable?

_____

Location 5: _____

Who potentially touched your vegetable?

_____

Now imagine that vegetable is not a cucumber or corn (or another vegetable you enjoy). Imagine it's a drug. In most cases, there are no federal guidelines for drugs. Who touched it? Who handled it? Do you even know that the drug you're using is pure? How do you know that pot isn't laced with heroin or cocaine? How do you know that pill is what you think it is? How can you be sure? Write down how you can know what you're doing is pure.

_____

_____

_____

_____

_____

Why would someone in the illegal chain care about you and your safety? How can you be sure that what you're doing is safe? Describe your thoughts, and if there is any way to know for sure:

_____

_____

_____

_____

_____

So, you've grown it yourself or it's a prescription drug that you're abusing. How can you be sure that mixing the drug with alcohol is safe? What steps can you take to ensure your safety? Can you REALLY be 100 percent sure that this is safe?

_____

_____

_____

_____

_____

Myth #3: Doing Drugs Is No Big Deal

Did you know that certain drug convictions can mean NO more federal financial aid? Did you know that people who have gotten federal aid who get convicted of drug charges can be forced to pay back the amount they used before the drug conviction? Wouldn't that suck (once you came down from your high)?

Did you know that students get high to avoid dealing with the BS that's part of life?

Did you know that a kid just died from huffing for the very first time?

Did you know that students die EVERY year from doing drugs? And many more are hospitalized without it ever being reported?

Drugs might not seem like a big deal to you, but they are to cops, administrators, res life staff, parents, significant others, and people you hurt while doing them. A felony charge, a call home from the school, or getting expelled is a big deal.

So, why do students do drugs? My answer: because they have a hard time dealing with life (i.e., emotional and social risks). If you turn back to the risk-taking exercise in the beginning of this workbook, you can find other ways to deal with life and take on the tough challenges that come with becoming an adult. But, getting back to the myths, doing drugs is hardly a good thing. What are some negative results that can happen as a result of drug use/abuse? List five:

1. _____

2. _____

3. _____

4. _____

5. _____

What are positive results?

1. _____

2. _____

3. _____

4. _____

5. _____

For all the positive results, what are alternative, legal, and safe ways to get the same results without doing drugs?

1. _____

_____

2. _____

_____

3. _____

_____

4. _____

_____

5. _____

_____

✎ Naked Journal #101: A Drug Report

It's time to do some research and really get to know your favorite drugs. Do a report using information from a trusted source (that would be a government agency or medical clearinghouse, not a good friend who does a lot of drugs) to find out the following information about three drugs.

Here's what you need to find out: 1) a brief description of the drug 2) street names 3) effect of the drug 4) risks of the drug 5) statistics and trends 6) what surprised you about your findings.

Naked Self-Exam Fourteen

Just in Case...

Rate using a scale of 1–10.

1 = Not true → 5 = Somewhat true → 10 = Doesn't get any truer

_____ I'm concerned about my safety on campus.

_____ I will NEVER be a victim of sexual assault.

_____ I'm never happy with my body image.

_____ Everyone is more attractive than me.

_____ Nothing bad will ever happen to me.

_____ I feel completely safe walking home alone at night.

_____ I am confident I will achieve my dreams.

_____ I feel depressed or lonely most days.

_____ I have a hard time sleeping at night.

_____ I've never been happier.

_____ Nothing excites me in life.

_____ As soon as I lose weight I'll be happy.

_____ I love helping other people.

Naked Exercise #102

The Truth about Sexual Assault

There isn't a sexual assault survivor in the world who thought it would happen to her (or him).

Most people think, "It can never happen to me." But sexual assault happens. It happens to sober people and it happens to people who drink or to people who do drugs. It happens at loud parties and it happens on quiet dates. It happens on big public campuses and it happens at small private schools. It happens.

Should this ever happen to you (whether you're a man or woman), the common reaction is to blame yourself. NEVER do this. One thing survivors have in common is that it is NEVER the survivor's fault. NEVER NEVER NEVER NEVER NEVER.

NEVER forget that.

Five Reasons Sexual Assault Is NEVER the Survivor's Fault:

1. _____

_____

2. _____

_____

3. _____

_____

4. _____

_____

5. _____

_____

Now that you know it's NEVER your fault, the next goal is to minimize the risks.
Think about your typical behavior when you go out (or stay in) with friends and drink. What can you do to minimize your risks? Check the box that applies in the following scenarios:

	Never	Sometimes	Frequently
I know everyone in the "group" who I'm drinking with.	☐	☐	☐

Why this matters: _____

	Never	Sometimes	Frequently
I let other people bring me drinks from the kitchen, keg, or bar.	☐	☐	☐

Why this matters: _____

	Never	Sometimes	Frequently
I open my own canned drinks.	☐	☐	☐

Why this matters: _____

	Never	Sometimes	Frequently
I let other people hold my drink while I go to the restroom or elsewhere for a few minutes.	☐	☐	☐

Why this matters: _____

	Never	Sometimes	Frequently
I set my drink down when I'm tired of holding it	☐	☐	☐

Why this matters: _____

	Never	Sometimes	Frequently
I typically trust other people.	☐	☐	☐

Why this matters: _____

	Never	Sometimes	Frequently
Date rape drugs are used on and around my campus.	☐	☐	☐

Why this matters: _____

	Never	Sometimes	Frequently
Incidents of rape are reported or known about on my campus.	☐	☐	☐

Why this matters: _____

	Never	Sometimes	Frequently
I am concerned that someone will put something in my drink.	☐	☐	☐

Why this matters: _____

	Never	Sometimes	Frequently
My friends and I pay attention to each other's drinking, how much we've had, and our condition.	☐	☐	☐

Why this matters: _____

	Never	Sometimes	Frequently
My friends and I stop each other from drinking too much.	☐	☐	☐

Why this matters: _____

	Never	Sometimes	Frequently
My friends and I keep an eye out for each other when we are at a party or bar drinking.	☐	☐	☐

Why this matters: _____

	Never	Sometimes	Frequently
My friends and I don't allow each other to leave with someone (whom we know or don't know) when we are really drunk.	☐	☐	☐

Why this matters: _____

And remember, even if you do everything you can to minimize risks, there's still a chance that this can happen. The most common rape is acquaintance rape. Should you ever think that you are a victim of rape or attempted rape, here's a national hotline you can contact to reach out for help:

RAINN: Rape Abuse and Incest National Network
Website: www.rainn.org
Hotline: 1-800-656-HOPE

True or False

1. Most sexual assaults are committed by acquaintances, not strangers.

    True or False

2. If you are too drunk to consent to having sex, it's still rape.

    True or False

3. Sexual assault crisis counselors are always available to help.

    True or False

The answer key: All TRUE

Your Local Contacts and Resources

Contact name: _____

Phone number: _____

Contact name: _____

Phone number: _____

Contact name: _____

Phone number: _____

✎ Naked Journal #102: It's NEVER the Survivor's Fault

I spend a lot of time in *The Naked Roommate* talking about how survivors of sexual assault are NEVER to blame. No matter what—NO ONE ever has the right to sexually assault someone. Write a short essay about why it's NEVER the victim's fault. Run through a list of possible reasons why a survivor might think it's his or her fault and explain why it's NEVER that person's fault. Feel free to share these with me via the Naked Roommate online community at: www.NakedRoommate.com and on Facebook at www.Facebook.com/TNRFanPage.

Naked Exercise #103

Exposing the College Eating Disorder

If you see someone who you think has an eating disorder, don't just look the other way or make comments. Help that person.

Afraid your eating disorder from the past might resurface? Ready to address an eating disorder you think you might already have? Eating disorders aren't fundamentally about eating; they're about a sense of personal control—or rather lack of control. Food becomes the means by which you take charge of something in your life, whether it is your body size, prompting attention from people around you, or just knowing that you and you alone can determine how much or how little you eat, and whether you let it nourish you or cause you to suffer.

If you think you may have an eating disorder (or know that you do), in what areas of your life do you not feel in control?

_____ Academics—my classes are hard, I'm not doing well, and I don't know how to get help.

_____ Time—I don't have enough time to study, work, hang out with friends, and just relax.

_____ Lifestyle—I don't have time or the ability to eat well or work out. I just eat what I can, when I can, and whatever's easy. I want to exercise but I'm always too tired and I don't have time to go to the gym.

_____ Family—my parents don't understand what college is like and they're expecting too much from me.

_____ Friends—I don't really have anyone I'm close to here and I feel lonely and isolated.

_____ Romance—I just can't seem to find anyone to date. No one is interested in me and I haven't been asked out.

_____ Future—I have no idea what I want to do when I finish college. I don't even know what I'm doing in college. I can't think past tomorrow. I haven't found my purpose in life.

There are many steps you can take to gain control in each of the areas where you are feeling helpless.

For difficulties with academics, time management, and the future, review the following tips (and activities in this book that relate to those tips. Maybe you skipped them the first time around, or need a little refresher). For taking charge of your social life and friend network, review Naked Exercise #10. Romance concerns, issues, and ideas are addressed in Naked Exercise #91. Parent problems, turn to Naked Exercise #6.

For lifestyle concerns, know that you are not alone. College presents a major shift in how your day-to-day life plays out in many ways. It is common for it to wreak havoc on your body and mind. So take some time to focus on whatever it is that is making you uncomfortable or downright unhappy. If you are feeling less than ideal about your body, identify exactly what things you would like to change.

_____ I would like to lose weight all over. Ideally, I would like to weigh _____ pounds less than I do now.

_____ I would like to gain weight; I am too skinny.

_____ I would like to be more muscular.

_____ I would like to have a flat stomach.

_____ I want my butt and my thighs to be smaller.

_____ I want to look "built."

_____ I want more curves.

_____ I want to wear a size _____.

_____ The person who embodies the look I want is _____.

(NOTE: If you just wrote the name of a hot celebrity, be aware that this hot celeb might be working 24/7 to look that way. That person doesn't have class, exams, and other things to do other than working out. Looking that way is that person's job. So pick me. I'm in good enough shape. That will be much less work.)

Given the rest of your previous answers, it is time to make a plan for how you can get help for your unhealthy and self-destructive behaviors, and accomplish those changes in your body in a healthy way. If you or someone close to you believes there is the possibility you could have an eating disorder, make an appointment at your school's counseling center. It is imperative that you work with a professional to deal with the mental and physical elements of your disorder.

If you suffer from a poor body image due to an unhealthy lifestyle, the best place to start is by connecting with your campus activity center or gym and finding a personal trainer and nutritionist who is on staff. Check out your campus website and list that information here.

Campus gym hours: _____ Weight room: _____

Pool: _____

Nutritionist name and contact information:

_____

_____

Personal trainer name and contact information:

_____

_____

P.E. classes offered that I am interested in taking:

_____ Aerobics (all over body trimming and weight loss)

_____ Weight training (toning, firming, muscle building)

_____ Yoga (all-over body trimming and weight loss, toning, peace of mind)

_____ Kickboxing (aerobic exercise)

_____ Dancing (aerobic exercise, body toning)

_____ Spinning class (aerobics, toning legs, butt)

_____ Sports (tennis, racquetball, basketball, swimming)

Discuss with the nutritionist and trainer what your goals should be.

Body weight: _____ BMI: _____ Waist: _____ Hips: _____

Arms: _____ Chest: _____

Daily calorie intake: _____ Daily fat grams: _____

Daily carbohydrates: _____

How often should you work out and in what ways?

_____

_____

If you have only a limited amount of time, what is the most effective workout?

_____

_____

Also create a nutrition plan that works with your college lifestyle. Ask the following questions:

If you have a meal plan for the dining hall, what are the recommended ways to eat what they serve?

_____

_____

If you live at home or cook for yourself, where can you get recipes for healthy, easy-to-fix meals?

_____

_____

What are good, filling snacks that you will enjoy and that give you energy?

_____

_____

What is the best way to deal with a "splurge"—when you indulge in a favorite that's not on the list?

_____

_____

The Student Counseling Center is also a good resource for when you are feeling overwhelmed and out of control, regardless of the reason.

Student Counseling Center location and contact information:

_____

_____

✎ Naked Journal #103: The Body Image

If there is one thing about your body that you could change, what would it be? Why would you want to change it? How would life be different? Now, imagine that you couldn't change it. How could you change how you see it so that it can be turned into an asset instead of a problem? How can you make life different with what you have?

Naked Exercise #104

Depression and Mental Health Issues

The happiest part about depression is that most people who get help can get better.

Did You Know?

- 65 percent of new students reported feeling lonely or homesick. (Source: Higher Education Research Institute 2010)
- 45.2 percent of college students reported feeling that things were hopeless at some point during the past twelve months. (Source: ACHA-NCHA fall 2011 report)
- 86.2 percent of college students reported feeling overwhelmed because of all they had to do. (Source: ACHA-NCHA fall 2011 report)

As I mentioned in the beginning of this workbook and throughout *The Naked Roommate*, life in college is 90 percent amazing and 10 percent difficult, but when the 10 percent becomes so difficult that it interferes with your daily life, it's a problem. When you start to exhibit the following symptoms, it might be more than 10 percent tough. Here are the symptoms of depression. Over the last two weeks how often have you experienced these?

Rank using a scale of 1–14.

(1 = one day over the last fourteen days → 14 = fourteen days over the last fourteen days)

_____ Persistent sad, anxious, or "empty" feelings

_____ Feelings of hopelessness and/or pessimism

_____ Feelings of guilt, worthlessness, and/or helplessness

_____ Irritability, restlessness

_____ Loss of interest in activities or hobbies once pleasurable, including sex

_____ Fatigue and decreased energy

_____ Difficulty concentrating, remembering details, and making decisions

_____ Inability to sleep, early-morning wakefulness, or excessive sleeping

_____ Overeating, or appetite loss

_____ Thoughts of suicide, suicide attempts

_____ Persistent aches or pains, headaches, cramps, or digestive problems that do not ease even with treatment

Other things that don't feel right:

_____

_____

_____

NOTE: Also refer to the list of depression symptoms in Tip #100 in *The Naked Roommate*.

If you're just too depressed to care about anything in this Naked Exercise, or you know someone who is too depressed to care—or wouldn't even know what I just said because he or she sleeps all the time, doesn't go to class, and has lost interest in the world—call the counseling center. Yes, even for someone else. If you know about it, it's your business.

If you are worried about yourself—or someone else—but aren't sure what to say to the counseling center, begin by filling out the following information and then get help as soon as possible. Most campuses have free or inexpensive services to help. Getting help isn't a sign of weakness; it's a sign of strength and courage.

List what symptoms you've been feeling from the previous list.

_____

_____

_____

Share anything else you've done or experienced that has filled you with regret, made you uncomfortable, sad, or disappointed in yourself.

_____

_____

_____

When did you start feeling these emotions?

_____

_____

_____

What have you done to get yourself help?

_____

_____

_____

Can you talk to your parents? If not, why not?

_____

_____

_____

Are you reluctant to get help? If so, why are you reluctant to get help?

_____

_____

_____

People you can talk to to get help (remember the people in your corner from Naked Exercise #9):

1. _____

2. _____

3. _____

4. _____

5. _____

Support groups, clubs, or organizations on campus that can offer additional support:

1. _____

2. _____

3. _____

4. _____

5. _____

Where to go on campus to get help:

Office: _____

Phone number: _____

Contact name: _____

Appointment time: _____

✎ Naked Journal #104: Getting Help

Think about the times you've helped people to feel better about a problem. Share how it made you feel to help them. Now share a problem that you've been battling and how it felt to reach out to have someone help YOU. If you haven't reached out for help, then use this as an opportunity to reach out and write about the experience.

Naked Exercise #105

The U of No Regrets

Some of the most difficult moments in life can become some of the best moments in life. You just have to be willing to look inward, look outward, and move forward. That's what college (and life) is about.

As you go through your college experience, appreciate that you can only make well-thought-out decisions based on the information you have at this moment in your life. So much of the learning experience is going through the experiences themselves...Instead of beating yourself up when a decision doesn't go as planned, take ownership and learn from it. Having been there and done it will allow you to do it all over again and do it differently.

Things I Did This Year That I Wish I Had Done Differently (Regrets):

1. _____

   _____

2. _____

   _____

3. _____

   _____

Now, for each regret you wish you did differently, record what you learned from the result and how the unintended outcome has created new opportunities.

1. _____

   _____

2. _____

   _____

3. _____

   _____

See? Ultimately those things that you initially might have labeled REGRETS, really can be labeled IMPORTANT LESSONS that will help you make better choices and live a more satisfying life in the future!

✎ **Naked Journal #105:** Naked Regrets

Look back to one experience that has happened to you during your first year in college. Pick an experience that was seemingly negative. Explain how this once difficult experience helped you to make discoveries about yourself and the people around you. Be sure to explain the experience in detail before sharing the lessons learned.

Naked Exercise #106

A Look Back in Time

Remember when you started this workbook you filled out ninety things you were looking forward to experiencing this year in college? Turn back to that page and review what you were looking forward to experiencing in college. Pick four things that you were looking forward to that turned out to be VERY different than you expected. Pick two that turned out better than expected and two that turned out not as good.

The expectation: _____

The reality: _____

What surprised you: _____

How you were able to get through it: _____

What you learned from it: _____

_____

What you would do differently the next time:

_____

_____

_____

* * *

The expectation: _____

The reality: _____

What surprised you: _____

How you were able to get through it: _____

What you learned from it: _____

_____

What you would do differently the next time:

_____

_____

_____

* * *

The expectation: _____

The reality: _____

What surprised you: _____

How you were able to get through it: _____

What you learned from it: _____

_____

What you would do differently the next time:

_____

_____

_____

* * *

The expectation: _____

The reality: _____

What surprised you: _____

How you were able to get through it: _____

What you learned from it: _____

_____

What you would do differently the next time:

_____

_____

_____

✎ Naked Journal #106: Naked Reflection

Time to reflect and take a look back at an amazing year of highs, lows, and everything in between. When you look back at the 90 things you were looking forward to about life in college, what jumps out at you? Are there items that seem silly in retrospect? What's missing from your list that should have been there? What surprises you? How does it feel to look at the past having experienced so much? Focus on one or two items on your list that had the most powerful effect on you, and explain.

The FINAL Naked Exercise: Naked Exercise #107

Insert Your Tip Here

This is your time to impact the lives of countless other students. Please take a second to share your tip and story for future editions of *The Naked Roommate*.

First start with the tip. Then finish with a story. Then title it. Then send it to me (address is on the next page). You might read it in the next edition of *The Naked Roommate* and see a corresponding exercise for it in the next edition of this workbook. Or, you can share your own idea for an exercise. That would sure make it easier for us.

The Tip

_____

_____

_____

The Story

_____

_____

_____

_____

_____

_____

```
Email to: Harlan@HelpMeHarlan.com
Subject: Naked Roommate Tip 5th Edition

Or post your tips and stories online
in the discussion area forums at:
www.NakedRoommate.com
www.Facebook.com/TNRFanPage
```

As promised, here are two more risk-taking worksheets for you to complete.

The Risk-Taking Project

Extra Pages

Preparing for the Risk

1. Define one risk you're going to take

Explain the risk you will take and your plan of action for taking this risk.

_____

_____

_____

_____

2. Possible obstacles

List three potential obstacles standing in the path to achieving your desired outcome.

1. _____

2. _____

3. _____

3. Preparing for obstacles

From the list of potential obstacles, list one action that you will take to help overcome each anticipated obstacle. Use the resources, support services, and people on and off campus to help you prepare for your risk.

1. _____

2. _____

3. _____

4. People in your corner

Who are the people who you can enlist to support you, guide you, and help you navigate through this particular risk (think of a boxer who enters the ring and the people in the boxer's corner helping him or her win)?

1. _____   4. _____

2. _____   5. _____

3. _____   6. _____

5. Expectations

Write a one-paragraph summary of your desired outcome for this particular risk.

_____

_____

_____

_____

_____

The Risk-Taking Results

This is where you get to share what happened. Remember, just having taken this risk is a HUGE success. Celebrate! You did it!

1. Outcome of your risk

Explain how the risk unfolded in detail.

_____

_____

_____

2. Your reaction to the results

Explain your feelings and how you reacted before, during, and after the risk.

_____

_____

_____

3. Evaluating the results

Did you achieve your desired outcome?

_____

Did your risk-taking go as planned or not as planned?

_____

_____

_____

Why didn't it go as planned? Why did it go as planned?

_____

_____

_____

What advice or guidance did you receive from the people in your corner?

_____

_____

_____

Was this advice and guidance helpful? If so, how? If not, why not?

_____

_____

_____

What surprised you the most about your risk-taking experience?

_____

_____

_____

What did you learn from this experience?

_____

_____

_____

If you take this risk again, what will you do differently the next time?

_____

_____

_____

* * *

Preparing for the Risk

1. Define one risk you're going to take
Explain the risk you will take and your plan of action for taking this risk.

_____

_____

_____

_____

2. Possible obstacles

List three potential obstacles standing in the path to achieving your desired outcome.

1. _____

2. _____

3. _____

3. Preparing for obstacles

From the list of potential obstacles, list one action that you will take to help over-come each anticipated obstacle. Use the resources, support services, and people on and off campus to help you prepare for your risk.

1. _____

2. _____

3. _____

4. People in your corner

Who are the people who you can enlist to support you, guide you, and help you navigate through this particular risk (think of a boxer who enters the ring and the people in the boxer's corner helping him or her win)?

1. _____   4. _____

2. _____   5. _____

3. _____   6. _____

5. Expectations
Write a one-paragraph summary of your desired outcome for this particular risk.

_____

_____

_____

_____

_____

The Risk-Taking Results

This is where you get to share what happened. Remember, just having taken this risk is a HUGE success. Celebrate! You did it!

1. Outcome of your risk
Explain how the risk unfolded in detail.

_____

_____

_____

2. Your reaction to the results
Explain your feelings and how you reacted before, during, and after the risk.

_____

_____

_____

3. Evaluating the results

Did you achieve your desired outcome?

_____

Did your risk-taking go as planned or not as planned?

_____

_____

_____

Why didn't it go as planned? Why did it go as planned?

_____

_____

_____

What advice or guidance did you receive from the people in your corner?

_____

_____

_____

Was this advice and guidance helpful? If so, how? If not, why not?

_____

_____

_____

What surprised you the most about your risk-taking experience?

_____

_____

_____

What did you learn from this experience?

_____

_____

_____

If you take this risk again, what will you do differently the next time?

_____

_____

_____

This Workbook is Now... OVER!

Pencils and pens down!

We hope you've enjoyed working on this workbook. Hopefully it wasn't too much work. As for the work you did do, we hope it was worthwhile. Should life in college ever get difficult or present uncomfortable challenges, know that you always have this workbook to help you work through the tough stuff and maximize the best college has to offer.

As always, we are open to your feedback and suggestions to make this workbook feel like little or no work. If there's something you loved, or something that could be better, please send a note and let us know what we can do to help create THE best naked college experience for you.

Thank you!

Harlan & Cynthia

The Naked Roommate Online

Find resources, participate in online discussions, read advice, and share your feedback. Connect with *The Naked Roommate* online:

- Website: www.NakedRoommate.com

- Facebook: www.Facebook.com/TNRfanpage

- Twitter: @NakedRoommate

The Naked Authors Online

Connect with Harlan:

- Website: www.HelpMeHarlan.com

- Facebook: www.Facebook.com/HelpMeHarlan

- Twitter: @HarlanCohen

- YouTube: www.YouTube.com/HarlanCohendotcom

- Email: Harlan@HelpMeHarlan.com

Connect with Cynthia:

- Email: Cynthia@college-by-design.com

Author Speaking Events

Keynotes, Workshops, and Live Events

Harlan Cohen is a nationally recognized speaker who has presented on hundreds of campuses across the country. Harlan delivers keynotes, facilitates workshops, and can be found participating in a wide variety of events. He can host your:

- College night event
- Conference keynote
- Graduation keynote
- Parent programs (high school and college)
- High school programs (sophomores, juniors, and seniors)
- Professional development workshop (for high school and college professionals)

Cynthia offers a wide range of professional development services for college and high school professionals.

For more information on Harlan's events and Cynthia's professional development services visit:

www.HelpMeHarlan.com/speak.html
www.HarlanCohen.com

The Instructor's Guide and Training on Your Campus

Interested in using *The Naked Roommate* book and workbook in the classroom?

There's now a *Naked Roommate Instructor's Guide* with a framework to help staff implement The Naked Roommate First Year Experience program. For more information on the guide or professional training in the classroom, contact:

Sourcebooks

(800) 432-7444 (toll-free)
(630) 961-3900 (phone)

Ask for academic sales.

Or

Help Me Harlan! Productions

Email: academicsales@helpmeharlan.com

About the Author:
Harlan Cohen

Harlan Cohen is the author of five books, a professional speaker, and one of the most widely read and respected male syndicated advice columnists in the country. Harlan is a *New York Times* bestselling author of the books *Getting Naked: Five Steps to Finding the Love of Your Life (While Fully Clothed and Totally Sober)* (St. Martin's Press), *The Naked Roommate: And 107 Other Issues You Might Run Into in College* (Sourcebooks), *The Naked Roommate: For Parents Only* (Sourcebooks), *Dad's Pregnant Too!* (Sourcebooks), and *Campus Life Exposed: Advice from the Inside* (Peterson's).

Harlan is a contributor to *Chicken Soup for the Teenage Soul III* and has been featured as an expert offering advice in the *New York Times, Wall Street Journal Classroom Edition, Real Simple, Seventeen, Psychology Today*, and hundreds of other newspapers and publications.

King Features Syndicate distributes Harlan's Help Me, Harlan! advice column worldwide. Harlan is a frequent guest on television programs across the country and has been a guest on hundreds of radio programs. Harlan is a professional speaker who has visited over four hundred college campuses. He is an expert who addresses teen issues, college life, parenting, pregnancy, dating, relationships, sex/no sex, rejection, risk taking, leadership, women's issues, and a variety of other topics. Harlan is the founder of the websites www.NakedRoommate.com, www.NakedRoommateForParents.com, www.GettingNakedExperiment.com, www.DadsPregnant.com, and www.HelpMeHarlan.com. He is the producer, lead singer, and musician on his album *Fortunate Accidents*. He lives in Chicago, Illinois, with his wife and two young children. In his spare time he goes through the exercises in the *Naked Roommate* workbook on an endless loop.

About the Author:
Cynthia Jenkins

Dr. Cynthia Jenkins has been engaging college freshmen for more than twenty years! With a bachelor of science degree in psychology and a PhD in human development and communication sciences, she began her career teaching in her favorite field. She has since expanded that role to include developing, managing, and teaching a First Year Experience course at the University of Texas at Dallas, writing a college study skills text, and traveling to colleges across the country to train FYE instructors on teaching an engaging college success course. She served as Director of Undergraduate Advising, Associate Dean of Students, and Assistant Vice President for Student Affairs at UT Dallas, where she worked with Residential Life, Freshman Living Learning Communities, New Student Programs, Parent & Family Programs, the Sophomore, Transfer, and Senior Year Experiences, and Student Volunteerism. In addition to working with Harlan on the Naked Roommate First Year Experience program, she is the owner and founder of Cynthia Jenkins Consulting and works with high school students to create their college paths. Contact her at Cynthia@college-by-design.com.

The Naked Roommate: And 107 Other Issues You Might Run Into in College

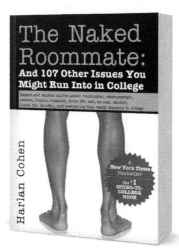

- The #1 going-to-college book
- Required reading on college campuses across the country
- More than 300,000 copies in print

"Advice columnist Harlan Cohen's *The Naked Roommate: And 107 Other Issues You Might Run Into in College* is a friendly, funny, and wise guide to making the most of college."

—Sarah Lindner, *American-Statesman*

"If *The Naked Roommate* existed when I went to college, I would have devoured every page before I stepped foot on campus."

—Linda J. Sax, Associate Director of The Higher Education Research Institute and Director of the CIRP Freshman Survey

"Fun and fact-filled, *The Naked Roommate* is an excellent resource for the college-bound high school graduate."

—*College 101*

"I might not yet know which institution I think best for my daughter, but I now know which book I will pack in her suitcase as she begins her college journey."

—Judith B. Greiman, President of the Connecticut Conference of Independent Colleges

Used as Required Reading on College Campuses across the Country

"The laughter and real-life honesty of the book's presentation helps students realize that their experiences are not unique to them and that everyone is in the same boat."

—Beverly Dolinsky, VP Student Affairs, Endicott College

"[*The Naked Roommate*] doesn't recommend excessive drinking, illegal drug-taking and random sexual hookups, but it recognizes that such things happen in college and offers sensible tips about what to do if you or your friends get in a jam."

—Charles McGrath, *New York Times*

"★★★★★ (Five Stars)...The most useful guide [on college life]."

—*The Daily Orange* (Syracuse University)

"For anyone who wants to know what college students really encounter, but has no idea what to expect."

—Josh Sanburn, Editor in Chief, *Indiana Daily Student*

The NAKED Suite of Products

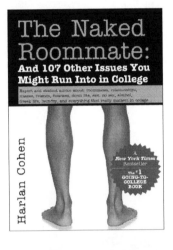

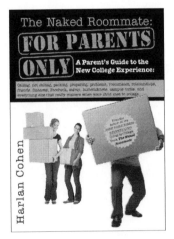

The Naked Roommate

The Naked Roommate's First Year Survival Workbook

The Naked Roommate First Year: The Complete College Transition Guide

The Naked Roommate Instructor's Guide

The Naked Roommate: For Parents Only

The Naked Roommate speaking tour

The Naked Roommate professional training (live seminar for instructors using the book as a First Year Experience text)

For more information on the NAKED suite of products, visit
www.NakedRoommate.com

A New Book for Parents of College Students by Harlan Cohen

Check out Harlan's new book for parents. Think of it as "The Naked Parent" but with a title more acceptable to their eyes. Harlan delivers the latest facts, stats, tips, and stories from parents, students, and experts from across the country to equip parents with everything they need to know to help their children (and themselves) have the best possible college experience.

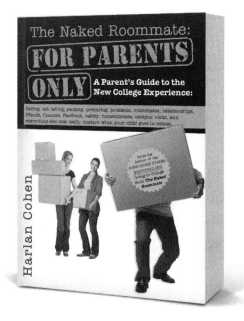